ENGLISH LEGAL SYSTEM

Questions and Answers Series

Series Editors   Margaret Wilkie and Rosalind Malcolm

Titles in the Series

Other titles in preparation

BLACKSTONE'S
LAW Q&A
QUESTIONS & ANSWERS

ENGLISH LEGAL SYSTEM

SUSAN McKENZIE
MA, LLM (London) MSI Arb,
Barrister of Inner Temple, Advocate and Solicitor, Singapore, Principal Lecturer in Law at Advanced Law Tutors, Singapore

S. KUNALEN
LLB (Hons) (London), LLM (London) (Mark of Distinction)
Barrister of Lincoln's Inn, Advocate and Solicitor, Singapore, Principal Lecturer in Law at Advanced Law Tutors, Singapore

OXFORD
UNIVERSITY PRESS

OXFORD

UNIVERSITY PRESS

Great Clarendon Street, Oxford OX2 6DP

Oxford University Press is a department of the University of Oxford.
It furthers the University's objective of excellence in research, scholarship,
and education by publishing worldwide in

Oxford New York

Auckland Cape Town Dar es Salaam Hong Kong Karachi Kuala Lumpur
Madrid Melbourne Mexico City Nairobi New Delhi Shanghai Taipei Toronto

With offices in

Argentina Austria Brazil Chile Czech Republic France Greece
Guatemala Hungary Italy Japan South Korea Poland Portugal
Singapore Switzerland Thailand Turkey Ukraine Vietnam

Oxford is a registered trade mark of Oxford University Press
in the UK and in certain other countries

Published in the United States
by Oxford University Press Inc., New York

A Blackstone Press Book

British Library Cataloguing in Publication Data

A record for this book is available from the British Library

Library of Congress Cataloging in Publication Data

Data applied for

ISBN 978-1-85431-533-5

9 10

Typeset by Montage Studios Limited, Hormonden, Kent
Printed in Great Britain
on acid-free paper by
the MPG Books Group, Bodmin and King's Lynn

Contents

publishers' staff who have been
ιamely, Alistair MacQueen and
ιk Susan's parents, Joy and Stan
ʹe would also like to thank Paula
ιcerning the writing of this book
ȝ this Q&A.

tended our classes over the years.
ιging of views over such matters
ther there was such a thing as the
ɔnderment amongst Singaporeans
and Wales are unpaid volunteers,
ϸehave in the police station etc.
Sometimes the debates became very heated but it was all really great. Thank
you and bless you.

Susan McKenzie
S. Kunalen
May 1996

Table of Cases

Table of Statutes

1 Successful Study Techniques

SYLLABUSES FOR ENGLISH LEGAL SYSTEM

English legal system is unlike other subjects such as contract, tort, criminal law or constitutional law where the syllabuses are roughly the same whichever university or institution you are attending. Syllabuses for English legal system vary from university to university. We concentrate on core areas that would appear on most syllabuses. One point that you should check is that the topic of police powers may be on your university's constitutional law syllabus rather than English legal system. Other titles for the English legal system are English legal process, English legal method, or an introduction to law or principles of law.

WHO IS THIS BOOK FOR?

This book is written for LLB students but it would also be relevant to the A level student who is aiming for a good grade and for all other courses where there is an English legal system content.

SUCCESSFUL STUDY TECHNIQUES

English legal system should be an enjoyable subject to study and you should get involved by thinking of why the legal system operates in the way that the legal system does and then consider ways in which it could operate more effectively.

We feel that the most effective way to study English legal system is by regular enthusiastic attendance at classes consistently over the course of an academic year with a teacher who is interested in the subject and is capable of bringing the subject alive.

This Q&A book is a back-up to proper studies and is designed to do the following:

(a)   Give you an additional source of research material.

(b)   Give guidance on how to answer questions.

Many universities are now moving to a style of question that requires more evaluative analysis. Students would be expected to think about the nature of the English legal system in terms of purposes and functions, openness and rigidity.

You are expected to develop over the course the following:

(a)   Independent thought.

(b)   Critical analysis.

(c)   Basic information

APPROACH TAKEN IN THE SUGGESTED ANSWERS

Some of the suggested answers are approached in an in-depth manner, which may be slightly longer than can be completed in an exam. This is so that the treatment of a particular area can be fully explained. You would summarise down a bit in the real exams. Also there is a view that if you learn more, there is a certain drop in the memory, so that in the actual exams you will have more than enough to write.

We give law report citations for cases and bibliographical details of books and articles mentioned so that you can follow up the references but in real exams you would not be expected to remember and give such references.

REAL SUCCESS

Successful studying is not just about passing exams and acquiring bits of paper. It is about whether in 10 years' time and for the rest of your life you will still be following some of the debates that take place about the English legal system or the legal system of whichever country you live in. Maybe you would be making a contribution as a practitioner of law or as a politician.

Be inspired by the examples of great persons. They used their studies of law to think about what should be reformed and they were instrumental in achieving that later on, for example, Lord Lester of Herne Hill QC, when a student, thought it unsatisfactory that the courts were not able to consult *Hansard*, the record of Parliamentary proceedings, to determine the intention behind a statute. Years later he was able to argue for change and achieve it in *Pepper* v *Hart* [1993] AC 593. When studying the law of contract as a student, Lord Denning thought that some of the rules concerning consideration were unjust and was able to influence the law when he was a judge.

Use this time as a student usefully to think about the law and how it should be reformed. How you are inspired as students can make a difference. As a lawyer, as a judge, as an academic, as a politician, you may be able to influence the future development of the law in a meaningful and constructive way.

2 Access to the Civil Justice System

INTRODUCTION

The English legal system has two main branches: the civil justice system dealing with civil disputes and the criminal justice system dealing with the enforcement of the criminal law. Each has its own court structure although there are some overlaps. The main civil courts of trial are the High Court and the county courts. The main criminal courts of trial are the magistrates' courts and the Crown Court. At the appeal stage there is one Court of Appeal but with two divisions: the Civil Division and the Criminal Division. There is a further appeal court namely the House of Lords. For European Community matters there is ultimately the European Court of Justice.

The court system exists for the resolution of disputes and to provide justice. There is no other justification for such a system. Therefore the court system should be structured in such a way that it carries out this function in the most efficient and effective way.

The civil court system has developed for the resolution of civil disputes. However, it has some problems such as whether people know that they have a legal problem and even if they do whether they can afford to use the civil justice system. These problems may be analysed by considering how accessible the civil justice system is. The lack of accessibility comes under the heading of 'unmet legal needs'. Actual access to justice is a weak point in the civil justice system. Successive government-appointed committees have tried to wrestle with ways to improve access to justice, for example, the Civil Justice Review in the 1980s and Lord Woolf's civil justice inquiry in the 1990s. One of the factors that has prevented an adequate solution has been resistance by the legal profession because of vested interests.

Access to justice includes a consideration of how the civil justice system works as a whole, the court structure, alternatives to a formal resolution of a dispute, funding of legal services and those who carry out legal services. All of this is connected to assessing how accessible the justice system is.

QUESTION 1

Justice is open like the doors of the Ritz Hotel. To what extent is justice accessible?

Commentary

This question requires a consideration of how accessible justice really is. This is the key issue facing the civil justice system. The reference to the Ritz Hotel is a reference to the high cost of legal proceedings. This is not acceptable and it has to be considered how justice could be made more affordable and accessible for everyone.

Suggested Answer

Lord Woolf has stated that although the court system is a good system no one can afford it. Neither the State nor the public can afford it.

The Lord Chancellor, Lord Mackay of Clashfern has stated that justice is priceless but it must not be too pricey if it is to be accessible. To be accessible, 'it must be affordable to the individual both as taxpayer and litigant' (Shimizu lecture entitled 'Litigation in the 1990s' (1991) 54 MLR 171).

Access to justice includes access to legal services and to the institutions that provide legal remedies — the courts, tribunals and alternative dispute resolution (ADR).

A system of justice is very necessary for the civilised resolution of disputes but if the people with disputes cannot afford to use the justice system then it fails to carry out its purpose and cheaper alternatives must be developed.

The factors which increase the cost of legal proceedings include:

(a)   the complexity of the legal system which forces users to employ lawyers,

(b)   the adversarial nature of procedures, with oral hearing and cross-examination,

(c)   the expenses of expert witnesses.

The principle that costs follow the event, which means that generally the loser pays the winner's costs, is a deterrent to plaintiffs.

The barriers to justice need to be broken down. The solution was thought to be legal aid and legal advice schemes. This is State funding being made available to pay for litigants' legal costs. However, provision of legal aid is limited and fewer and fewer people qualify for it.

Another suggestion has been that procedures should be simplified. So far this has had only limited success, and research has found that, even where procedures were intended to be user friendly, litigants in person were still at a disadvantage. Within the county court there is a simplified procedure for claims under £3,000 which is intended to be used by litigants in person. Lawyers are not banned but are discouraged because costs cannot be recovered from the losing party. However, research conducted for the Civil Justice Review found that litigants who were represented in the small claims proceedings had a greater chance of success. The Civil Justice Review came to the conclusion that it would be better to have experienced lay representatives than inexperienced litigants in person conducting cases. Therefore the Civil Justice Review recommended that lay persons should have a right of audience in small claims proceedings. This has now been allowed since the Lay Persons (Rights of Audience) Order 1992. Thus the experience of small claims proceedings is that there are limits to the extent that procedure can be simplified. Alternatives to lawyers include Citizens' Advice Bureaux and law centres but the distribution of these throughout the country is very uneven.

Conclusion

A justice system that operates like the Ritz Hotel is clearly unacceptable.

Cost is the problem with the civil justice system but nobody has yet been able to provide a solution to the problem. It seems that there must be a package of measures including informal procedures, lay advisers, and effective State funding. Costs will always be a question that has to be dealt with. Unless there are free or highly subsidised legal services then the law will never be genuinely open to all.

Lord Woolf believes that if the alternative is between not going to court because you cannot afford a Rolls Royce system and accepting a rough and ready model that does not produce such a refined product then he would prefer the latter.

QUESTION 2

Assess the problems facing the legal system today with regard to civil matters.

Commentary

This question follows on from question 1. The problem is a civil justice system that is open like the Ritz Hotel and provides a costly Rolls Royce service. This is fine for those who can afford it or who qualify for legal aid but the majority of the population cannot, so this question considers what attempts have been made to find solutions to this problem.

When considering the legal system everything in the system should be considered, including the courts, lawyers, judges, dispute resolution techniques, and making the system affordable to both taxpayers and users.

Suggested Answer

The major problems facing the civil justice system today are high costs which affect accessibility. What causes high costs and what can be done to reduce them?

The court of trial is a central and fundamental part of the legal system. Even if few persons pursuing civil legal disputes actually take their disputes to trial, the process is still there as a last resort which can be used as a threat to induce people to settle. The British style of trial has been a single uninterrupted event with the parties' evidence unfolding before the court. This method developed at a time when there was greater use of trial by jury and it was difficult to reconvene a jury after an interruption.

Trial has the following benefits:

(a)   There is oral argument. This is where the issues are heard and considered and one can be satisfied that the judge has really understood the issues. Also points can be more effectively emphasised before the judge.

(b)   Cross-examination is the best means of getting at the truth, especially where important facts are deliberately concealed and distorted.

(c)   Trial is usually final.

These are great strengths but they have the drawback of being expensive. Trial takes a lot of preparation and generally needs expensive lawyers. Thus it would seem that within the existing framework it is difficult to reduce costs dramatically.

There have been various attempts to do something about high costs, for example, the introduction of legal aid. This was an attempt to make the system affordable to the ordinary person. Legal aid is available for most court proceedings except defamation, small claims proceedings and most tribunals. The State, not the client, pays the lawyer, though if the client wins then the Legal Aid Fund has a first charge on the costs and damages recovered. The problem with legal aid is that it does not try to reduce the costs of the system but acts as a relief to subsidise those who are less well off. The costs are still there but the State pays them.

Therefore there needs to be a major re-examination of the court procedures. One of the reasons for setting up the Royal Commission on Legal Services, which deliberated from 1976 to 1979, was a concern about anti-competitive practices in the legal profession and the costs they were generating, in particular, the costs of litigation.

The view that was accepted by the Royal Commission was that the costs of litigation were due to the procedures and if the procedures could be simplified then costs would be reduced. The government's response to this was to set up the Civil Justice Review in 1985.

The Civil Justice Review 1985 to 1988

The Civil Justice Review correctly identified the problems of civil justice as being 'delay, cost, complexity and lack of access to justice'.

The Review had been set up by the then Lord Chancellor, Lord Hailsham of St Marylebone. He was very traditional in his approach and supported the Bar and its restrictive practices. His ideas centred around the existing court system and the Bar's exclusive rights of audience in the higher courts and therefore he would have wanted the court structure to be divided between the High Court and the county court. Thus it could not be expected that the Civil Justice Review would provide radical solutions. Its proposals merely amounted to procedural tinkering.

The main change resulting from the Civil Justice Review is an increase in the jurisdiction of the county courts. Section 1 of the Courts and Legal Services Act 1990 gave the Lord Chancellor the power to make jurisdiction orders. The High Court and County Courts Jurisdiction Order 1991 has given the county court unlimited jurisdiction in contract and tort. All personal injury actions below £50,000 now have to start in the county court. Other matters below the value of £25,000 should start in the county court. Other changes include a recommendation to increase the jurisdiction of the small claims proceedings and also to permit lay persons rights of audience in certain proceedings in the county court.

Lord Woolf's Civil Justice Inquiry 1994 to 1996

In March 1994 the government appointed Lord Woolf and a team of litigation experts to carry out a fundamental review of civil court procedure. One of the tasks that they were given was to reduce the rules of court and combine the two separate rule books for the county court and the High Court into one. This would create a simple unified procedure with a single set of rules.

Lord Woolf's view of the 1980s Civil Justice Review was that all it amounted to was polishing of the existing system, i.e., that it was not radical and did not really solve any of the problems, namely, costs, complexity, delays and ensuring access to justice. He did, however, agree that moving a lot of High Court work to the county courts was a substantial improvement. Lord Woolf's view is that the role of the judge has to be looked at.

Lord Woolf has made it very clear what he is hoping to achieve and in 1995 he published a report entitled *Access to Justice*.

The main recommendations that the report made are as follows. Lord Woolf has identified that the problems are due to the uncontrolled nature of the litigation process and from the absence of clear judicial responsibility for managing individual cases. There should be judicial management of cases with procedural judges who should be appointed to take control of cases at an early stage. They would fix timetabes for hearings and set ceilings on costs. They would also appoint expert witnesses and reduce the number of documents before the court.

It has also been recommended that there should be a Citizens' Advice Bureau at every large court centre. It is hoped that the Bureau could help many litigants with preparation so that people would only need legal help for the actual hearing.

Lord Woolf proposes a new way of allocating cases into three tiers:

(a)   Claims under £3,000. These will fall within the expanded small claims jurisdiction. A judge will no longer have to find a case to be 'exceptionally' complex in order to consider it inappropriate for the small claims procedure. Personal injury claims for less than £3,000 will be automatically allocated to the fast track (see (b)) unless a party wishes to utilise the small claims procedure and the court agrees to this.

(b)   Claims under £10,000. These will be allocated to a new 'fast track' leading to a trial within a short period of time, which is hoped to be 20 to 30 weeks. The trial would last for a maximum of half a day. Discovery and oral evidence from lay witnesses will be limited, expert oral evidence excluded, and costs fixed. Cases will be heard by district judges at local courts convenient for the parties. However, this procedure will be appropriate only for straightforward cases. Claims under £10,000 which involve complex issues of law or fact, or issues of public importance or interest, or a significant amount of oral evidence, or multiple parties will be allocated to the multi-track (see (c)).

(c)   Claims over £10,000. These will be allocated to a new 'multi-track' which covers both the High Court and the county court. More complex cases will be heard by a High Court judge.

A procedural judge will decide the track.

The whole aim of Lord Woolf's proposals is to improve access to justice.

The success of Lord Woolf's proposals will depend on commitment and cooperation on the part of the judiciary and court officials, members of the legal profession and litigants as well as financial resources provided by the government.

The concerns that have been expressed about Lord Woolf's report are that the proposals will change the role of the judge, experts and discovery in a way that is outside the English tradition and is much too European. The proposed new system depends on the calibre of the judges who are not yet adequately trained in case management. However, others are of the view that Lord Woolf did not go far enough when he did not suggest that the traditional divisions of the High Court should be merged or that the county court and the High Court should be amalgamated.

Another development that has taken place in the 20th century has been the development of specialised tribunals. They have some presumed advantages over the courts:

(a)   They are so informal that it is believed that professional representation is not needed. A tribunal should safeguard the interests of the unrepresented applicant so that a case with merit will succeed however inexpertly presented.

(b)   By concentrating on a particular area of the law a tribunal should develop knowledge and therefore, even though the tribunal chairman and the lay assessors are not of the same calibre as a judge, their expertise in their own area of the law should lead to good-quality decision-making.

(c)   No legal aid is generally available because tribunals are speedy and informal so that the lay person can present his or her own case.

However, research evidence has refuted these claims and shown that the emphasis on informality may lead to certain misconceptions about informal procedures, namely:

(a)   small does not necessarily mean simple, and

(b)   there are limits with informality — tribunals are still bound by the law, regulations and precedent.

In an industrial tribunal, for example, an applicant must still bring his or her case within the regulations and prove the factual situation with evidence. All applicants have to be able to show a legal right or an entitlement, and a respondent must prove a defence. Unrepresented persons have difficulty in identifying the facts relevant to their cases. They may fail to produce necessary evidence through ignorance of what is required. The reality is that the tribunal model does not eliminate the need for professional assistance. It could be that the problem is the underlying approach which is based on the adversarial model, i.e., opposing sides with an adjudicator.

Conclusion

The overriding problem with the civil justice system is cost. It is currently a system where there needs to be legal assistance because the average person is not capable of being an effective litigant in person. There have been attempts to create user-friendly procedures, such as tribunals and the small claims procedure, in which legal assistance is not needed. However, research has shown that those who have legal assistance in those jurisdictions are at an advantage. It has been thought that the underlying basis of these jurisdictions is still too adversarial and that this must change if there is to be real progress. Lord Woolf's idea is that judges should cease to leave case presentation to the parties and should actively manage cases themselves.

QUESTION 3

In addition to action in the courts, there are other ways in which legal disputes may be resolved. Analyse critically the different ways (including through the courts) in which such resolution may be achieved.

Commentary

Resolution by the courts is not the only method of dispute resolution. In fact if the parties can resolve their own differences then there is no need to use the court system. Likewise if they agree to use an alternative to the courts then they can do so. This question requires consideration of both the traditional methods of dispute resolution and also some of the main alternatives.

The following answer mentions the existing court documents. Lord Woolf's report, *Access to Justice*, proposes that the court documents be retitled and be the same whether the action is proceeding in a county court or the High Court. All pleadings would be called a statement of case, with specific documents called a claim, a defence and a counterclaim. In the most common type of proceedings the statement of case could even be a computerised questionnaire.

Suggested Answer

Traditional Way of Resolving a Dispute

The traditional way of resolving a dispute is to commence an action in the courts. Depending on the value of the claim, this would be either in the High Court or a county court. If the value of the claim is less than £3,000 then it would come within the jurisdiction of small claims proceedings.

In the High Court an action is started by the issue of a writ and in a county court by way of a summons. In outline the procedures are as follows. The plaintiff's pleadings have to be served in the form of a statement of claim for High Court proceedings and particulars of claim in a county court. This document sets out the claim. If the defendant is defending then a defence will be served. When all the court documents setting out the claim have been served, close of pleadings will take place. The next stage is pre-trial matters, including discovery. This is where each side discloses to the other the existence of the documents relevant to the case. Then the case is set down for trial, a hearing date is taken, and then trial. At the end of the trial judgment will be given to the winning party and if the loser does not willingly pay then enforcement proceedings will be taken.

However, in the majority of cases, often before a court action is started, the parties try to resolve their differences by negotiation. Negotiation is where the parties try to resolve their dispute and come to an agreement on how the matter is to be dealt with. If these negotiations break down then the party who has the cause of action may decide to commence court proceedings. Even after the court action has started the parties could reach a settlement. A settlement can be reached without involving the use of court procedures but it can also be used together with the court procedures. For example, the most costly aspect of the court process is the actual trial so the threat of going all the way to trial puts pressure on the other side to settle because of the costs involved. Also there is the fear of the costs principle that the loser pays the winner's costs. These are powerful reasons causing the parties to settle and almost all cases actually settle without going to a full trial. Research for the Royal Commission on Civil Liability and Personal Injury 1978 (the Pearson Commission) showed that only 1 per cent of personal injury claims reach court each year.

Commercial Contracts

The parties to a commercial contract may have set out in the contract that disputes are to be resolved by a reference to arbitration. The parties appoint an independent adjudicator. The arbitration process is similar to a court hearing but it is in private and is not part of the court system. This is not generally cheaper than the courts because the arbitrator will want a fee but the business community prefer this method because they can ensure that a specialist is the arbitrator, it is in private and the dispute can be settled quickly. An arbitrator's award is binding.

Small Claims Proceedings and Tribunals

Small claims proceedings within the county court deal with claims up to £3,000. The procedure is intended to be more informal with the aim of providing a cheap, simple mechanism for resolving small-scale consumer disputes.

Another way of resolving disputes is tribunals. They were set up to deal with certain areas of the law, for example, employment cases go to the industrial tribunals. These bodies are supposed to be informal with no restrictions on rights of audience. However, in practice there is an advantage if one is represented by a legally experienced person. Further, tribunals deal with specialist areas of the law and so can only be used if the problem falls within that specific area. Tribunals have been popular with governments in the twentieth century, presumably because it is believed that parties to tribunal proceedings do not need legal representation so that there is no need for comprehensive legal aid provision.

Alternative Dispute Resolution

The term 'alternative dispute resolution' or ADR is used to describe various ways of resolving disputes without resort to courts or tribunals. This would include arbitration, conciliation and mediation. In conciliation and mediation a third party is introduced into the negotiations to help the parties reach an agreed settlement. The techniques are used when the parties have failed or are unlikely to reach a settlement on their own. ACAS, the Advisory, Conciliation and Arbitration Service, is an administrative agency which helps to resolve disputes between management and trade unions. It was set up by the Employment Protection Act 1975 and is funded by, but independent of, government.

The aim of both conciliation and mediation is that an existing relationship can be saved and can continue. Mediation and conciliation are similar. Mediation involves an impartial independent third party who attempts to bring the parties to agreement but who does not put forward solutions. Conciliation may go further and attempt to effect a reconciliation and give a non-binding opinion.

The problem with these types of ADR is that both parties have to consent to their use; they are not legally binding and if one party refuses to cooperate then they cannot be used.

Conclusion

The traditional method of dispute resolution has been through the courts. Although court proceedings may be issued, the vast majority of cases do not result in trial but are settled before that stage. Therefore the court system is still an important way of getting parties to resolve their disputes. Arbitration has developed as an alternative to the courts but because arbitration is similar to court proceedings the search is still on to find quicker, cheaper and simpler forms of dispute resolution. However, the role of ADR as a method of dispute resolution is a permanent feature of the civil justice process. In January 1995 the Lord Chief Justice published *Practice Direction (Civil Litigation: Case Management)* [1995] 1 WLR 262 which requires each party to lodge with the court a completed pre-trial checklist which asks whether the parties have discussed the possibility of ADR. The parties are asked to consider whether some form of ADR might resolve or narrow the issues in question.

QUESTION 4

Assess the working of small claims procedures. Assess why they were developed and consider to what extent they have achieved their aims.

Commentary

The small claims procedure in the county court is yet another attempt to make access to justice a reality for claims involving small amounts of money. There needs to be an assessment of the extent to which this has been achieved.

The raising of the small claims jurisdiction from £1,000 to £3,000 is a key recommendation in Lord Woolf's report *Access to Justice*. This increase was widely backed by consumer groups. Small claims arbitration in their view offers ordinary people with ordinary claims against builders, retailers and holiday companies a chance to get justice cheaply and quickly.

Suggested Answer

The setting up of small claims proceedings was a response to a need to find cheaper ways for resolving disputes for matters concerning small monetary amounts. The pressure for such a procedure came from consumer groups who had started private schemes to show to the government the need for such procedures. These private schemes stopped when small claims proceedings were set up in the early 1970s. With effect from 8 January 1996 the jurisdiction has been increased from £1,000 to £3,000. The only exceptions to this procedure will be claims for possession of land or personal injury claims exceeding £1,000.

Almost every consumer will have a problem with a faulty purchase at some time. Therefore there is a large potential demand for an accessible, cheap and easy procedure for resolving consumer disputes. Further if small claims proceedings were really effective then the fact that there is such a system to fall back on would mean that traders would try to resolve their problems more quickly and sympathetically.

The small claims procedure is part of the work of the county court. The process is entitled 'arbitration' to emphasise that the objective is to allow litigants to represent themselves at a hearing where their ignorance of procedure and the nature of the proceedings will not be a handicap. The hearing should be informal and the formal rules of evidence and procedure do not apply.

However, research has shown that the majority of users in these courts are not ordinary persons acting on their own or if they are then they are at a disadvantage for so doing when they are up against represented or experienced defendants. No legal aid is available for small claims proceedings.

Research has shown that the process is too complex and does not overcome most people's fear of litigation. District judges differ considerably in their willingness to be helpful to unrepresented litigants. In addition, in *Chilton* v *Saga Holidays plc* [1986] 1 All ER 841 the Court of Appeal held that the underlying procedure is adversarial and the district judge cannot disallow cross-examination. The Civil Justice Review recommended that the district judge should have the power to disallow cross-examination.

In fact the Civil Justice Review realised that judicial training has a crucial role in promoting informality in proceedings which is necessary if a litigant is to be able to bring a case without representation. Investigative hearings require greater judicial skill, because district judges must put litigants at ease, explain complex legal rules clearly and prevent litigants from going off the point without appearing biased.

As a response to the Civil Justice Review's finding that experienced litigants were at an advantage compared to inexperienced litigants, the Civil Justice Review recommended that there should be a right to representation by a lay representative. By s. 11 of the Courts and Legal Services Act 1990 the Lord Chancellor was given the power to introduce orders permitting lay persons rights of audience in small claims proceedings. He permitted this by the Lay Persons (Rights of Audience) Order 1992.

Small claims proceedings seem to work best with straightforward claims. There have been concerns that certain types of actions are very difficult for an unrepresented person, for example, housing claims, including claims for disrepair. Further in many of these claims the claimants have poor linguistic skills.

The Law Society has attacked such an approach and has argued that by not exempting disrepair claims from small claims, tenants will not receive legal costs when they win which is not an improvement of access to justice. The reality will be that many tenants with good claims just will not be able to pursue them. Lawyers have also made similar claims with regard to personal injury actions.

Further research published in 1995 by Professor John Baldwin of Birmingham University's Institute of Judicial Administration has found that the small claims proceedings are dominated by small firms and professionals. Two hundred and sixty two litigants were interviewed. The conclusion from the interviews was that there are ignorance and misconception about the court procedures and the actual procedures vary from one court to another.

The research found that it was difficult to translate a common-sense view into a legal framework and that it is difficult for lay persons to assess legal validity. The research found that the small claims procedure was dominated by small firms and managers pursuing claims against each other. It is professionals that mainly present cases and there are not many working-class people who do. If it was the intention that the poor should assert their rights, then the research found that they do not. Professor Baldwin has suggested that 'court surgeries' should be introduced because there has to be something at the court to help people. Legal advice should be available at specified hours during the week. (See 'Which people's court?' (1995) 139 SJ 1195.)

This research highlights the deficiencies in the small claims procedure which clearly have not been rectified by the Civil Justice Review recommendations and the changes made pursuant to that report. The Birmingham research shows that the small claims procedure is neither accessible nor responsive to the litigant. It is still not reaching the less well educated and the less confident prospective litigant. This research was sponsored by the Lord Chancellor's Department.

Need for Publicity

Another problem has been the lack of awareness about the existence of small claims proceedings. The small claims procedure can only resolve peoples' problems if they know about it. Thus there must be continual efforts to promote the county court as a place where ordinary people can go to sort out consumer and other disputes. Effective publicity would include posters on local buses, press and radio items, displays in shopping centres and libraries. Posters and leaflets in advice centres alone are not good enough because they only reach people who already think they might have a remedy.

Conclusion

Even if a person successfully pursues a small claim this does not mean that automatically the person gets paid. It is still necessary to enforce the judgment which means more proceedings. In addition to simpler court proceedings there is a need for simpler and more effective enforcement proceedings.

The small claims procedure is a very necessary procedure in principle. It has its defects and these should be addressed. The solution would seem to be greater training for the judiciary in case management because control by the judge is the most effective way of proceeding in small claims. If Woolf is really able to change the culture of the courts then one of the beneficiaries will be small claims. This is because the success of small claims has always depended on how helpful the judges are prepared to be. A system of justice aimed at the needs of unrepresented litigants will only work if there are real major changes from traditional court practices and the right attitude from court staff and judges.

3 Legal Services, Lawyers and the Courts

INTRODUCTION

The traditional providers of legal services have been barristers and solicitors, and most of this chapter will concern these professions.

In an examination:

(a)   There could be a question purely on the legal profession. See questions 1, 2 and 3 in this chapter.

(b)   The role of the legal profession with regard to legal aid and other methods of funding might be considered — see chapter 4. Question 4 in that chapter explores whether it would be better to have a National Legal Service instead of relying on solicitors in private practice.

(c)   A question might consider the role of lawyers in increasing access to justice and reducing unmet legal needs. See chapter 2.

(d)   The way rights of audience were changed and the loss of the conveyancing monopoly are case studies in the law reform process and can be used as examples of law reform.

QUESTION 1

Solicitors and barristers are an unnecessary burden on the legal system.
Discuss.

Commentary

This question requires a critical consideration of the contributions that both
solicitors and barristers make to the legal system but also a consideration of the
extent to which some of their practices act as a burden on the system.

Suggested Answer

Development of the Legal Profession

The two branches of the legal profession developed as a result of the structure
of the courts and a belief that those who argued cases before the courts should
belong to a society that could control the professional discipline of its members.
The Bar in earlier centuries was the only profession that the judges felt had been
able to achieve that level of organisation. This is why the judges gave the Bar
their exclusive rights of audience in the superior courts.

It was legislation setting up the county courts, namely, the County Courts Act
1846, that gave solicitors rights of audience in the county courts. The Bar had
opposed this. However, by the twentieth century the Law Society had achieved
an organisation that could regulate professional discipline to an adequate level
and solicitors started to demand additional rights of audience, which was
resisted by the Bar.

Objectives of the Legal System

The legal system has developed to deal with two different types of legal
problems:

   (a)   Legal problems that are categorised as criminal.

   (b)   Legal problems that are categorised as civil matters.

This distinction has led to the creation of civil courts of trial and separate
criminal courts of trial.

Objectives of the Criminal Justice System

The objectives of the criminal courts are to ensure the conviction of the guilty and the acquittal of the innocent. The strength of the evidence implicating an accused will vary from case to case and some evidence may be unreliable, for example, confessions. Therefore the system has to provide a process by which the prosecution case can be tested fairly. The best test is some form of court hearing in which witnesses have to undergo cross-examination to see whether they can be believed. The British believe that the most effective way to do this is an oral hearing in the nature of adversarial proceedings open to the public. The adversarial nature of proceedings puts the burden of preparing the case on to the parties. The party who is best prepared has an advantage. Therefore the employment of lawyers will contribute to that advantage because it will be they who prepare and present the case. Therefore while the court proceedings have these characteristics lawyers are necessary.

Objectives of the Civil Justice System

The civil courts have different objectives to the criminal courts. The objectives of the civil courts are the resolution of disputes and providing access to justice. Civil procedure is also based on adversarial proceedings. Therefore again the party with the best prepared case will be at an advantage.

At the moment, with the exception of the small claims proceedings, only solicitors and barristers have rights of audience in the county courts and magistrates' courts. In the superior courts only barristers and solicitor advocates have a right of audience. Solicitor advocates are solicitors who have obtained a right of audience qualification in the superior courts.

Since the passing of the Courts and Legal Services Act 1990 the machinery is available to authorise non-lawyers to conduct litigation and advocacy services. The statutory objective (s. 17) is that a wider category of people should carry out these services. This it is hoped will lead to greater competition and mean that cheaper legal services will be offered. In another area, conveyancing, the advent of licensed conveyancers has been one of the reasons why conveyancing costs have reduced by up to 50 per cent. These developments show that there is still a need for providers of legal services but they may not necessarily have to be barristers or solicitors. Barristers and solicitors blame the high costs of litigation on the complex civil procedures and there continue to be attempts to simplify civil procedures. Lawyers have been blamed for the high costs of litigation. In Sir Thomas Bingham's 'Price of Justice' lecture 1994 he felt that there would only be meaningful reductions in litigation costs if there was court management to take control of the case from beginning to end. Lord Woolf has suggested that there should be court management with procedural judges setting costs ceilings and ensuring that the issues in dispute are identified and where possible trying to get the parties to settle. It is hoped that eventually the litigants themselves will do the bulk of the preparatory work. Up to now with the civil court system, as it is currently arranged lawyers have been necessary. If reform of civil procedure could ever be successful enough so that litigants in person could really do most of the preparatory work then lawyers might not be so necessary.

Lawyers' Contributions to the Legal System

Lawyers do make a contribution in that they have been instrumental in creating a greater awareness that persons may have legal problems through, for example, Accident Line. They have provided free services such as FRU (Free Representation Unit) and individually, for example, as volunteers in Citizens' Advice Bureaux. It also has to be realised that there is no career judiciary in the United Kingdom. Judges are appointed from the ranks of lawyers and the English judiciary has a good reputation for a strong legal ability which has been developed over many years of practice.

Unnecessary Burden

The organisation of the legal profession has been criticised in that there is unnecessary duplication. This should decrease with the advent of more solicitor advocates. If there are unnecessary costs then this is an unnecessary burden. If also the legal profession tries to thwart attempts to make proceedings less adversarial or tries to stop other professions or bodies from conducting litigation or advocacy then again the legal profession has become an unnecessary burden.

Conclusion

Nobody has seriously suggested that in the criminal justice system there are effective alternatives to barristers and solicitors. If there are any unnecessary burdens it is the artificial restrictions on solicitors but these have been resolved since December 1993 with solicitors being able to obtain Crown Court advocacy qualifications. These qualifications are still unnecessarily restrictive because there is much work in the Crown Court that is no different from magistrates' court work such as pleas in mitigation on guilty pleas.

Further nobody has seriously suggested that there should be changes from the present adversarial nature of proceedings for the criminal justice system. It is the procedures that need persons with legal expertise and therefore lawyers are best placed to provide such legal expertise.

With regard to civil proceedings lawyers are blamed for the high costs. Meaningful cost reductions may take place with court management. Also with computerisation it may be possible to devise ways in which lay persons could do more of the work. However, when informal procedures have been created such as in small claims proceedings research has shown that litigants in person are still at a disadvantage. One solution has been to permit lay persons rights of audience in small claims on the basis that this must be better than the inexperienced litigant in person. This would tend to indicate that legal assistance is necessary although it may not require a fully qualified lawyer. However, the problem with small claims and tribunals is that the underlying nature of proceedings is adversarial and this is why litigants in person still have problems. Court management is argued to be different because it changes the actual nature of the proceedings.

Further it is with regard to the civil justice system that the Lord Chancellor is of the view that access to justice need not necessarily mean access to lawyers and access to the courts.

QUESTION 2

Assess the significance of solicitors obtaining rights of audience in the superior courts.

Commentary

In principle solicitors have now finally achieved their ambition of being able to practise advocacy in the higher courts. This was the traditional territory of the Bar. Therefore the 'significance' that the question refers to is how this development will affect the Bar.

Suggested Answer

The Royal Commission on Legal Services (1976 to 1979) reported that the Bar should keep its exclusive rights of audience in the superior courts because this was in the public interest. This was never accepted by the Law Society and by the mid 1980s the bickering between the Bar and the Law Society had reached such a state that the differences were being described as 'Bar wars'.

To resolve these differences the Bar and the Law Society agreed to set up a committee to make recommendations about the rights of audience dispute. This committee was entitled the Committee on the Future of the Legal Profession (also known as the Marre Committee). However, this committee was split on the rights of audience issue and the Bar would accept no substantial changes.

The Lord Chancellor, Lord Mackay of Clashfern, used this as an excuse to say that if the profession could not resolve this problem then it was the duty of the government to step in. The end result was the Courts and Legal Services Act 1990 which provided a machinery by which the Law Society would be authorised to permit solicitors to obtain rights of audience. The machinery included the creation of the Lord Chancellor's Advisory Committee on Legal Education and Conduct consisting of a superior court judge who is the chairman, a circuit judge, two barristers, two solicitors, two persons experienced in the teaching of law and nine lay persons. This committee considers applications and then advises the Lord Chancellor and the four designated judges whether they should be accepted. The designated judges are the Lord Chief Justice, the Master of the Rolls, the President of the Family Division and the Vice-Chancellor. They all have to agree to accept any changes.

Section 17 of the Courts and Legal Services Act 1990 lays down the statutory objective and the general principle. The statutory objective is the development of legal services by making provision for new or better ways of providing such services and a wider choice of persons providing them, while maintaining the proper and efficient administration of justice. The reference to 'new' means alternative and the new services do not have to be better than existing ones.

As a general principle, whether a person should be granted a right of audience should be determined by reference only to whether he or she is qualified in accordance with the educational and training requirements appropriate to the court, and whether he or she is a member of a professional body that has rules of conduct with an effective mechanism for enforcing them.

It took until December 1993 before the Lord Chancellor and the designated judges were prepared to grant the Law Society's application but only for solicitors in private practice. The application concerning employed solicitors was referred back to the advisory committee for further consideration but was rejected by the committee in May 1995.

Solicitors' rights of audience on admission remain the same. After three years' experience a solicitor can apply for extended rights of audience. A solicitor must obtain a certificate of eligibility by proving sufficient lower-court experience. A solicitor has to obtain a separate advocacy qualification for the High Court and a separate one for the Crown Court. An applicant must demonstrate relevant experience and training and must pass a test in evidence and procedure. The test for the higher civil courts advocacy qualification covers evidence and procedure in the higher civil courts. The test for the higher criminal courts advocacy qualification covers evidence and procedure in the higher criminal courts. Having passed the relevant test the solicitor must pass the higher criminal courts advocacy training course and/or the higher civil courts advocacy training course where appropriate.

By May 1996 only about 400 solicitors had obtained Higher Court advocacy qualifications. Solicitors have failed to take up rights of audience in the higher courts in any substantial numbers. Cost, the time commitment and the perceived difficulty of the examination were given as reasons why there had not been a greater uptake.

However, this is still a very significant change because the Bar's monopoly has been broken. Clients will no longer be forced to employ a separate lawyer for higher-court advocacy. This has led to speculation about the Bar's long-term future because solicitors can now do work that was traditionally the Bar's preserve.

The conditions for obtaining these higher courts advocacy qualifications have proved restrictive for some of the big City law firms because they rarely do county court work. Large firms are worried that they will have to take on hundreds of county court cases just to get the ones that go to trial, and even then these would be a means to an end, namely, the qualification to appear in the High Court. However, it is thought that one benefit of the changes for the large firms is that law firms which offer advocacy training are likely to attract the best graduates because training contracts with advocacy may be seen as a better option than Bar pupillage.

The extent to which this affects the Bar will depend on how frequently solicitors exercise these rights. There is evidence that solicitors are starting to use their advocacy rights more often and with rights of audience in the higher courts available it is making it more economic for a solicitors' office to have an advocacy department.

The Bar has had to rethink its role since these changes. It is in a dilemma because if more solicitors exercise their rights of audience they will cut out the Bar as the client first goes to see a solicitor. If that happens the amount of work going to the Bar will reduce and the Bar will wither. If the Bar responds by dropping its no direct access rule then barristers would be no different from solicitors in reality and that would be fusion through the back door. The no direct access rule is that a client cannot instruct a barrister directly but must go through a solicitor. However, the Bar realises that it has to concentrate on its strengths such as being high-quality specialist referral advisers and the Bar will only survive if it can show that the public would get a better service with a barrister than with a solicitor.

The significance of the change has put a focus on considering whether the Bar has a useful purpose any more. Probably the answer to that is to let the market decide. Therefore the changes have meant an increase in competition.

Therefore the Bar will only continue in its present form if it continues to be useful. The utility at the moment is that smaller solicitors' firms are still heavily reliant on barristers for independent advice and advocacy work. However, solicitor advocates have set up their own association, the Association of Higher Court Advocates. Their stated aim is to do better than the Bar.

Conclusion

There is no doubt that solicitors obtaining rights of audience in the superior courts has had an impact leading to the Bar having to reconsider its position and to consider ways to improve the service it provides.

QUESTION 3

All rules and practices which restrict or limit the way in which a lawyer may choose to practise should be abolished. Discuss.

Commentary

The legal profession has always been described as a bastion of restrictive practices. This question requires a consideration of the extent to which some or all of these restrictive practices are unnecessary.

Suggested Answer

Main Restrictive Practices

The main existing restrictive practices are as follows.

Barristers have no direct access to the general public. There is a rule against barristers entering into partnerships with fellow barristers or anyone else. Barristers who are not in private practice but are employed only have rights of audience in the lower courts, i.e., county courts and magistrates' courts.

Solicitors do not have automatic rights of audience in the superior courts and have to obtain higher courts advocacy qualifications to do this. Further, solicitors canot enter into partnerships with barristers or other professionals except foreign lawyers. A solicitor not in private practice is an employed solicitor and cannot qualify for rights of audience in the superior courts.

Rationale for Restrictive Practices

There are various reasons for restrictive practices and these are:

(a)   To maintain standards.

(b)   To protect the public from dishonest and incompetent lawyers.

(c)   To ensure the quality of advocates in all the courts including the superior courts and to facilitate the smooth administration of justice and to ensure that judges can rely on the advocates.

(d)   To be able to give independent and impartial advice.

It is argued that when considering the structure of the legal profession there is a need to ensure high standards of professional competence and integrity which includes the need to avoid conflicts of interest, whether between client and practitioner or between one client and another. It is important to preserve the practitioner's independence and freedom from external pressures.

No direct access rule

The no direct access rule for the Bar makes it a referral profession. This rule means that the Bar is not directly competing with solicitors for the same work. Therefore when solicitors refer work to barristers they know that they will not lose the client. Further this role has the effect of making the barrister complementary to the solicitor in that the barrister handles the more complex work that a solicitor cannot deal with, and provides specialist legal opinion and advocacy. Abolition of the no direct access rule would effectively reduce the differences between barristers and solicitors and would amount practically to fusion. A believer in fusion would certainly want this restrictive practice abolished.

Partnership Restrictions

Barristers cannot enter into partnerships with other barristers. The argument in favour of this rule is that more barristers are available to appear on opposite sides in litigation which gives greater choice. This is more crucial in specialist areas of practice. Two barristers in partnership could not appear against each other because of their conflict of interest in sharing in the partnership profits. Also in a partnership the dominant partners decide what work they can take on, for example, some of the large City law firms have decided only to do corporate civil work.

However, the arguments against continuing such a restriction are:

(a) The partnership medium is good for corporate responsibility because the whole firm is responsible for the conduct of the case and for ensuring that the matter is dealt with properly.

(b) The partnership seems to be a better medium for the development of new entrants to the profession because they can receive a salary from the partnership.

Rights of Audience

Since the Courts and Legal Services Act 1990 a machinery has been provided by which solicitors can obtain rights of audience. The whole procedure has been severely criticised by former presidents of the Law Society as too convoluted and the resulting conditions for qualification too restrictive. Employed lawyers at the moment have not been allowed to qualify for rights of audience in the higher courts at all. This particularly affects the Crown Prosecution Service. The Bar refused to apply on behalf of employed barristers but the head of the Government Legal Service and the Director of Public Prosecutions (head of the Crown Prosecution Service) have applied on behalf of employed barristers. The Lord Chancellor's advisory committee rejected the applications in May 1995 by a majority of nine to eight and advised the Lord Chancellor not to approve the application. The nine who recommended rejection of the application were barristers, judges and some academics. Those in favour of it were six non-lawyers and two solicitors.

The Law Society has urged the Lord Chancellor to accept the minority's advice, as it feels that the majority's reasons are just excuses to keep the status quo and that the committee has considered wider policy grounds which is overstepping their mandate.

The majority said that allowing CPS lawyers to prosecute in the higher courts would be incompatible with the proper and efficient administration of justice because they did not believe that employed lawyers would have a sufficient degree of independence. There was a danger of prosecutors being 'prosecution-minded'. The majority also believed that so much work would be lost by independent advocates that there would be a serious diminution of choice for the public. The minority view was that lack of independence was an unsupported allegation and that allowing rights of audience to CPS lawyers would increase their accountability for key prosecution decisions. The Law Society claims it has not received any formal advice from the committee of the precise nature of any new objections to its application on these grounds and has not been given the opportunity, as required under the Courts and Legal Services Act 1990, to consider whether to amend its application to meet such objections. The CPS is not excluded from the Courts and Legal Services Act 1990 and therefore in principle should be allowed rights of audience subject to the conditions laid down in the Act. It is arguable that advice that CPS-employed lawyers should not be granted higher court rights of audience under any regulations or rules whatsoever lies outside the statutory remit of the committee.

The Bar has, however, welcomed the majority's view and urges acceptance of them. The Bar's attitude is that the reasons for not allowing Crown prosecutors rights of audience is because this is not a debate about maintaining some monopoly for the Bar, it is about ensuring in the more serious criminal cases that there are independent prosecutors who may be barristers or solicitors in private practice to act as an important check on the power of the State and to prevent abuse of that power. It is essential that a system of State prosecutors should not emerge. The Bar has argued that if civil servants are the prosecutors then there will be no restraint on their suppression of relevant information. They will not have counsel telling them to disclose it.

Therefore there are two diametrically opposite views, one that it is in the public interest for employed lawyers to have rights of audience which in principle Parliament accepted in the Courts and Legal Services Act 1990, the other that it is not. It is no surprise that it is the Bar taking the approach that it is not in the public interest because barristers have much to lose from Crown prosecutors having rights of audience in the superior courts.

Business Structures

Solicitors are not allowed to be partners in multidisciplinary partnerships. This is by the practice rules laid down by the Law Society. The arguments against such a development are that it may affect a solicitor's ability to give impartial and independent advice. Those who argue in favour of such a development claim that business clients need less protection than, say, individuals. The dangers of such a development are that it might lead to big multidisciplinary practices that concentrate on services to business clients and it may lead to a massive reduction of independent law firms who carry out a service that deals with the private client's problems especially in defending criminal charges.

The main reason against partnerships between solicitors and barristers must be that to allow this would lead to de facto fusion. However, as solicitors and barristers are legally trained then in principle there is no reason other than trying to keep the division going for maintaining such a rule. The Royal Commission on Legal Services argued in favour of an independent Bar because it means that barristers are available for use by all firms of solicitors and it provides access to legal expertise that might not have been available in any other way. The Royal Commission was of the view that only the largest firms of solicitors would be able to take into partnership enough barristers to cover a comprehensive range of specialism, leading to a concentration into the bigger practices and to reduce competition. Further that partnerships between barristers and solicitors would restrict clients' choice of barristers particularly in specialist areas of practice.

Conclusion

Restrictions should only remain if they are in the interests of the public and the proper and efficient administration of justice. There need to be rules which maintain standards, ensure the quality of lawyers and the quality of the legal services that are provided. Views differ as to what is in the public interest but it is necessary to take into consideration:

(a)   Relaxations of the restrictions between barristers and solicitors will result in some form of fusion.

(b)   Permitting multidisciplinary partnerships will change the nature of practice as a lawyer.

4   The Price of Justice

INTRODUCTION

This chapter is connected to chapter 2 on access to justice and chapter 3 on the way legal services are organised. Without legal aid, members of the public will not be able to afford legal services. However, there are severe inadequacies with the present arrangements and it is the inadequacies and the solutions to them that will be explored in this chapter. It has been recognised since the early 1960s that legal aid is not the complete answer because there are still unmet legal needs. The solution is no longer just legal aid but a much wider approach to publicly funded legal services. The last question of this chapter discusses the view that legal aid should be abolished and replaced by a national Legal Service which arguably could be a better management of resources than legal aid and might reach more persons.

QUESTION 1

Assess the role of legal aid.

Commentary

Legal aid has made an important contribution to alleviating a lack of access to justice. It has also played a crucial role in correcting the inequalities caused by the greater resources of the police and prosecution in the criminal justice system.

Suggested Answer

Legal aid was introduced with the aim of providing equal access to justice for the majority of the population and was originally intended to cover at least 70 per cent of the population. Although estimates vary, it is probably now covering less than 30 per cent of the population. Legal aid for civil and criminal matters should be looked at separately.

Civil Legal Aid

The Legal Aid and Advice Act 1949 created a system of civil legal aid. The scheme was intended to pay for the lawyers' costs and the general costs of preparation to help people bring or defend cases before the civil courts but not for tribunals. Applicants had to pass a means and merits test. Those with a disposable income or capital above certain limits had to pay a contribution. The merits test was designed to ensure that a case had a reasonable prospect of success before public money was spent on it. However, if a legally aided person won his or her case there was a statutory charge so that some of the money recovered or preserved was taken to pay for any costs of the action not met by the other party. In that sense, civil legal aid was a loan rather than a grant.

Legal aid was to be provided by solicitors in private practice. However, this meant that access to justice depended on whether a solicitor in the locality was prepared to open an office and undertake legal aid work. There have always been solicitors not prepared to undertake legal aid work. The Legal Aid and Advice Act 1949 even allowed the Law Society to run the legal aid scheme. This continued to be the position until the Legal Aid Board took over this role in 1989 pursuant to the Legal Aid Act 1988.

The Rushcliffe Committee (the Committee on Legal Aid and Legal Advice in England and Wales) was the body that considered the form that legal aid should take. Their conclusions formed the basis of the Legal Aid and Advice Act 1949. The Rushcliffe Committee had rejected a publicly run system based on the network of Citizens' Advice Bureaux which had developed during the Second World War. Despite this there was a revival of Citizens' Advice Bureaux and the creation of law centres in the late 1960s and early 1970s. The main push for these came because there were not enough lawyers providing services in areas such as social welfare law which included landlord and tenant, housing benefits, employment law, debt, immigration and welfare rights.

Citizens' Advice Bureaux and law centres concentrated on giving legal advice whereas legal aid is about representation and preparation for litigation. It was realised that there was a need for legal advice and some basic assistance like letter writing. This led to the introduction of the green form scheme in 1973. This allowed solicitors to conduct a short means test and provide immediate 'legal advice and assistance' on any matter concerning English law, though in the 1980s advice on wills and conveyancing was excluded. Assistance by way of representation (ABWOR) was created in 1979. This extended the green form scheme to cover certain proceedings in the magistrates' courts. ABWOR covers bail applications, pleas in mitigation, and representation at mental health review tribunals but not at other tribunals. In 1983 a duty solicitor scheme was introduced to help unrepresented defendants appearing before magistrates' courts and was extended in 1986 to provide free advice for people arrested and detained at police stations.

The Role of Legal Aid as Envisaged by the Legal Aid Board

The role of legal aid may change in the future. This is because the Legal Aid Act 1988 created a new framework for legal aid. A Legal Aid Board was created with the power to consider new or better ways of providing publicly funded legal services. The major innovation that has been introduced is franchising. This means that solicitors' firms have to apply for a franchise to be able to carry out legal aid work. In the future this will be the only way that solicitors' firms will be able to undertake work on a legal aid basis. The Board has argued that this approach improves the quality of work because only firms that can comply with the franchise stipulations will be able to obtain a franchise. However, with an open system of legal aid there are about 11,000 solicitors' firms able to do such work. It is predicted that when the system goes fully over to franchised firms only, there would only be about 3,000 firms having a franchise which would reduce the access points for legal aid. Also once there is a fully franchised system in operation the next development could be block contracting and competitive tendering, i.e., firms would then have to compete for particular types of work. Critics argue that these developments will lead to a very restricted access to legal aid.

Criminal Legal Aid

The major role of criminal legal aid is to provide assistance in preparing the case and providing representation for defendants in criminal proceedings. Criminal legal aid has made a great contribution because research has clearly shown that defendants who are not represented by a lawyer are more likely to be convicted and if convicted to get a stiffer sentence than they would have otherwise got if they had been represented. It can often mean the difference between conviction and acquittal, because the lawyer can see a defence to the charge which would not occur to the lay person.

The role of criminal legal aid is to ensure that, where the interests of justice demand it, a person charged with a criminal offence should have legal representation. To qualify for criminal legal aid the accused person has to satisfy a means test and an interests of justice test. Most defendants in the Crown Court receive criminal legal aid but they may have to make a contribution. However, in the magistrates' courts fewer defendants are legally aided.

The role of legal aid in criminal proceedings is not to further access to justice because the accused person is facing justice — an accused has no choice but to take part in the proceedings. Criminal legal aid contributes to the quality of criminal justice by providing equality before the law if the quality of the aid provided is comparable to the resources available to the prosecution. There have been concerns that in certain situations there have been some deficiencies with the quality of legal aid. The most well-known examples come from the miscarriage of justice cases, for example, the Birmingham six in which the defence were hampered because their forensic scientist was not able to carry out tests to prove his theory that persons who had handled playing cards would give the same test results as those handling explosives. Legal aid was not available to cover the costs of such tests. This might have made a crucial difference to the defence or at least as to how the case was viewed in later years. In *R v Callan* (1995) Michael Mansfield QC criticised the defence expert and made the point that if the defence were dissatisfied with their expert, the relevant legal aid authorities would not generally authorise the funding of another expert. *R v Callan* was a case of alleged murder. The case against the accused was that he had shaken a little girl to death. His defence was that she had fallen and that it was an accidental death. In prison he read up on the area and was able to show years later that she had died in circumstances consistent with his defence. The case of Stephan Kiszko showed that legal aid is generally not available after conviction to search for new evidence, which has to be privately funded. The evidence which proved his innocence only became available after his mother employed a private detective to unearth it.

Thus whilst legal aid covers basic legal assistance and representation in court, it has proved not always to be adequate for providing forensic resources.

Conclusion

There is no doubt that legal aid has played an important role in helping to further the objective of access to justice and equality before the law assisting litigants to pursue claims and to defend themselves.

In all types of proceeding legal representation gives a party an advantage. This is because lawyers are familiar with the court procedures, know how best to prepare and present a case, what points to raise, and what questions to ask.

QUESTION 2

Consider the contribution of conditional and contingency fees to access to justice.

Commentary

As the government is no longer prepared to commit unlimited resources to legal aid, alternative methods of funding have to be considered. The government's answer has been conditional fees. This question requires a consideration of their practical working. Conditional and contingency fees are another way of providing access to justice. However, the UK has not been prepared to accept the system of contingency fees used in the USA. It has to be considered whether conditional fees will be as effective as contingency fees in securing access to justice.

Suggested Answer

Sir Thomas Bingham, the Master of the Rolls, in his 'Price of Justice' lecture (Holdsworth Club, University of Birmingham, March 1994) stated that if it is not possible to provide a well-funded legal aid system then it is necessary to permit contingency fees. Thus the main driving force for the introduction of conditional fees has been the fact that a big proportion of the population are not eligible for legal aid yet fear suing because of the large amount of costs they would have to pay if they lost. This group of people have been described as being in the middle-income trap.

Therefore in 1989 the government issued a Green Paper entitled *Contingency Fees*. Although the paper was entitled *Contingency Fees* the government made it very clear that it was not in favour of full-blown American contingency fees but preferred the Scottish version known as the speculative action. The government was against contingency fees because it believed they could lead to an explosion in litigation which could lead to prohibitive insurance premiums and the demise of some industries and activities as a result of not being able to obtain insurance.

There is a contingency fee if a lawyer agrees to accept a client's case on the basis of receiving no payment if the case is lost, but some percentage or share of the award made by the court if the case is won. In a Scottish speculative action solicitors receive their normal taxed costs if the case is won, but nothing if it is lost. The problem with this Scottish system is that very few actions are funded on this basis because it is not very attractive to lawyers.

The main disadvantge of contingency fees is that they may result in a conflict of interest between lawyer and client. The lawyer will have a direct financial interest in the outcome of the case and will be unable to give the client impartial advice. The potential dangers are that:

(a)   The lawyer may be tempted to encourage the client to settle early to avoid the effort involved in fighting a case but this can be dressed up as avoiding the uncertainties of litigation.

(b)   The lawyer may concentrate on cases with a high nuisance value where the defendant is more likely to be forced into making an offer to settle.

(c)   The lawyer may be tempted to try to enhance a client's chances of success, perhaps by coaching witnesses or withholding inconvenient evidence.

It is argued that lawyers might be tempted to act unprofessionally but it is arguable that this can be controlled by professional discipline.

Other concerns are that contingency fees might lead to inflated claims so as to cover the fee.

The greatest advantage of contingency fees is that they are the key to the courthouse. They allow people to litigate who could not otherwise litigate. There is also an argument that says half a loaf of bread is better than no loaf.

Thus the government was prepared to accept a subtle variation of the American system know as conditional fees. The Lord Chancellor was given the power to introduce conditional fees by s. 58 of the Courts and Legal Services Act 1990. After long consideration these were finally introduced by the Conditional Fee Agreements Order 1995. Conditional fees work on the basis that if the client loses the lawyer will be paid nothing but if the case is won the lawyer can charge his or her normal fee plus an uplift. The lawyer would not have a direct interest in how much the client received but would be paid more to compensate for lost cases which resulted in no fees. The Lord Chancellor has emphasised that conditional fees are different from contingency fees because they relate to the actual work done and not to a percentage of damages awarded as in America. Competition between lawyers would ensure that the uplift was kept to a reasonable level. Critics have disputed this, arguing that conditional fees are a form of contingency fee and will generate all the perils normally associated with American contingency fees.

The Lord Chancellor initially wanted the uplift to be 20 per cent. Solicitors argued that this would not be a good enough incentive for the riskier cases. Therefore the uplift was finally agreed as up to 100 per cent. The Conditional Fee Agreements Order 1995 applies only to specified proceedings, namely, personal injuries, insolvency cases, proceedings before the European Commission of Human Rights and the European Court of Human Rights.

With regard to the problem of costs following the event and the loser paying the winner's costs the Law Society was able to negotiate with regard to personal injury claims an insurance scheme where one could insure against the risk of having to pay the other side's costs.

There have already been successful cases taken on a conditional fee basis. Examples of successful cases were reported in (1995) 92 (41) Gazette 1. A female lorry driver won £6,000 for a workplace accident and a pensioner who hurt her leg tripping on a pavement was awarded £2,000. The uplift in these cases was limited to 25 per cent of the damages, which is the Law Society's recommended maximum.

Lawyers are also reporting that conditional fees are being used for insolvency cases. They are proving to be an effective weapon against directors who run away from insolvent companies after stripping them of assets. This is considered to be more effective than the threat of disqualification.

Conclusion

Conditional fees are now a fact of life. They are good news for clients. They have been described as a real step forward in increasing access to justice for those not eligible for legal aid who had previously been prevented by fear of costs from pursuing legitimate claims. In the long run they will only continue to have public support if it is litigants and not lawyers who are seen to be the principal beneficiaries. Conditional fees might be bad news for hospitals, local authorities and other public bodies who are responsible for causing a large number of personal injury claims. These bodies might have to take meaningful steps to improve their procedures and improve public safety which would also be good for the public.

QUESTION 3

Unmet legal needs are a continuing problem. Should there be concern if such needs remain unmet?

Commentary

The existence of unmet legal needs is part of the problem of access to justice. It may be true that the total elimination of unmet legal needs is impossible but that is no reason for not trying. The main impediments to access to justice are:

(a) Not realising that the problem is capable of legal solution.

(b) Fear of costs.

Suggested Answer

Meaning of Unmet Legal Needs

There are unmet legal needs where people either do not know their legal rights or know them but are deterred from using them, for example, because they are frightened by the costs. There is also research that shows that some people find the image of some solicitors' firms off-putting and will not consult a solicitor because of this. Legal aid has never solved the problem because it does not cover the majority of the population and there is what is known as the middle-income trap where people are too wealthy to qualify for legal aid yet do not feel wealthy enough to afford litigation. Also even if you qualify for legal aid you have to be able to know about it or realise that you have a legal problem. If you do not know about legal aid or do not realise that you have a problem then legal aid can do nothing for you. It was to try to solve these problems of lack of knowledge and the approachability of solicitors that Citizens' Advice Bureaux and law centres were created. Although these bodies have been very successful where they exist they have never solved the problem because they are not available throughout the country and they lack resources.

In an opinion poll in 1993 a further reason for unmet legal needs was identified, namely, people do not want to sue friends or relatives.

Explanations for the Continuing Existence of Unmet Legal Needs

The main reasons for continuing unmet legal needs are costs and a lack of awareness that the problem is capable of legal resolution. The fear of costs is increased by the rule that the loser has to pay the winner's costs.

Reasons Why Unmet Legal Needs Matter

If high costs stop people litigating then justice is not being done in their cases which is an injustice. Access to justice is important because it is something that should be available in a country that considers itself to be civilised. Also it is needed to stop people taking the law into their own hands. Injustice is not acceptable in a civilised country. It also matters because access to justice is part of the principle of the rule of law. The rule of law is only properly upheld when there is equality before the law and equal access to justice.

Government's Attempts to Alleviate Unmet Legal Needs

The most substantial attempt to reduce unmet legal needs was the setting up of the legal aid system. It has made a substantial contribution but today because eligibility is so low the majority of the population no longer qualify. Citizens' Advice Bureaux and law centres were set up in the 1960s and 1970s to try to give more publicity to the availability of legal services and to provide legal advice. There are about 1,000 Citizens' Advice Bureaux and about 50 law centres. Law centres are mainly found in London and other major cities. The other reason why Citizens' Advice Bureaux were a necessary development was because they act as an invaluable filter into the legal system. They are also arguably more approachable than solicitors' firms, and law centres are often found in poorer areas where there are no or fewer solicitors' firms. So long as a person can identify that he or she has a problem, the advice worker can advise which would be the most appropriate agency to assist with that problem. The other benefit of law centres is that they can look at community problems in general (i.e., group problems) as opposed to just dealing with individual problems, for example, tackling a local authority over disrepair on a whole council estate.

Advice workers can deal with some of the problems, explaining legislation, filling in forms, making telephone calls, drafting letters or referring the enquirer to a specialist agency including a solicitor. A few Citizens' Advice Bureaux and other agencies provide representation before industrial tribunals and social security appeal tribunals which are not covered by legal aid.

Non-government Attempts to Alleviate Unmet Legal Needs

The Law Society accepts some collective responsibility to do what it can to improve access to justice. It set up the Accident Legal Advice Service (ALAS) in 1986. This was replaced by Accident Line in 1994. This includes a free telephone line which will tell callers the names of participating solicitors in the locality and a free half-hour interview to explore whether the person has a valid claim and qualifies for legal aid.

The aims of Accident Line are:

(a)   to make accident victims realise that they might have a claim,

(b)   to overcome their uncertainty about how to approach a solicitor, and

(c)   to allay their fears about possible costs.

Leaflets and posters about Accident Line are distributed to hospitals, doctors' surgeries and libraries.

The Law Society since the mid-1980s has allowed solicitors to advertise the services they carry out. This has led to a greater awareness of the services available from solicitors.

Further the Law Society has carried out advertising on behalf of all solicitors highlighting the benefits of using solicitors' services generally.

The Bar has developed the Free Representation Unit (FRU) which provides free representation before tribunals.

There are the individual efforts of lawyers prepared to carry out volunteer work, for example, volunteering to spend time giving free advice in Citizens' Advice Bureaux or other pro bono work.

There has been pressure from non-governmental organisations, for example, consumer organisations setting up private small claims courts to show their worth eventually leading to the government setting up small claims proceedings in the county courts. Consumer organisations are also part of the pressure for there to be low-cost legal services.

Consumer organisations produce reports that increase the debate on how to shape and fund legal services. The organisation Justice has produced reports suggesting alternative ways of providing funding, for example, the Contingency Legal Aid Fund (CLAF).

The organisation, Liberty, has created the Liberty Panel of lawyers who are prepared to take on cases free of charge referred to them by Liberty. They would be cases concerning human rights issues and would generally be test cases. The participating City law firms and barristers who have been instructed have been prepared to act on a pro bono basis.

Conclusion

There are two aspects to unmet legal needs:

(a)   Legal advice about whether there is a claim.

(b)   Pursuit of the case to trial.

With regard to the first point, because of solicitors being able to advertise the awareness of solicitors' services has increased. Also where they are available, Citizens' Advice Bureaux and law centres make people more aware. With regard to the second point, with the reduction of the availability of legal aid the problems of affording to pursue a case have got worse. Therefore the costs problem is something that the government has to tackle.

It can be argued that it is the government which is at fault for the continuing existence of unmet legal needs. This is because the most effective way of reducing such needs is a comprehensive legal aid system. The government has argued that spending on legal aid is too high and must be controlled. However, the government cannot ignore unmet legal needs because of political pressure concerning them. Therefore if this problem is to be really tackled then radical options need to be considered.

Radical options would include the adoption of contingency fees, a contingency legal aid fund and a National Legal Service.

Contingency fees are where a lawyer is prepared to act on the basis of no fee if the case is lost but would receive a percentage of the damages recovered if there is a win. The government has not been prepared to accept this method because of fears that it could lead to an over-litigious society. Justice's model is a contingency legal aid fund which works on the principle that the fund is in charge. Only approved lawyers would be allowed to undertake such work. The fund would pay for the lawyers' costs if the case is lost but would take a percentage of the damages if there is a win. However, somebody has to provide the funds initially and this is why the government has been reluctant to agree to the setting up of such a fund.

Another radical idea is the setting up of a National Legal Service. This would provide free or highly subsidised legal services and would be a public-sector solution instead of the haphazard private-sector approach to legal aid.

QUESTION 4

Is there a case for a National Legal Service, just as there is a National Health Service?

Commentary

This question requires a consideration of a radical new way of delivering legal services. Because of the strength of the professional bodies wanting a private-sector solution to the provision of legal services, the public sector is undeveloped. Yet a public-sector solution should be considered. There is already a public sector in existence in the form of Citizens' Advice Bureaux and law centres. They have had to develop because of the legal profession's reluctance to operate in some places such as poor inner-city areas and also with regard to disputes concerning small amounts of money where it is uneconomic to employ a lawyer. Also there are such areas as tribunal work where no legal aid is available so that generally solicitors do not carry out the work. This covers areas such as welfare law and industrial tribunal work. If the private-practice legal profession has failed to provide an adequate all-round service then there has to be another approach. The National Legal Service idea is something that should be considered. The comparison with the National Health Service is relevant. The National Health Service was being set up when the Welfare State was being created in the 1940s. Legal aid was conceived as the second prong of the welfare State, the legal equivalent of the National Health Service. However, the Law Society was able to persuade the committee considering the form of legal aid to take a private-sector solution. This has never been totally satisfactory and probably the most sensible solution would be a National Legal Service. The only problem is whether people of sufficient competence and motivation would be attracted to such a service and be prepared to stay with it.

It is not silly comparing a National Legal Service with a National Health Service. The Law Centres Federation has long argued that private practice by solicitors should be replaced in the long term by a salaried legal service. But if the comparison is health, than today there is a role for both private and publicly funded health services so the model should be that those who want to pay privately for legal services can go to a solicitor in private practice while those who cannot afford or want something cheaper can go to the National Legal Service. It is already recognised that law centres could play a major role in providing legal services. They are a public-sector solution and a National Legal Service could be built up from the existing law centre movement and the Citizens' Advice Bureaux. Back in the 1980s when the Efficiency Scrutiny Committee recommended that Citizens' Advice Bureaux should take over green form advice that was being carried out by solicitors in private practice, the Citizens' Advice Bureaux refused on the ground that they would not be provided with adequate resources for the job. Thus if the law centres movement and the Citizens' Advice Bureaux can be persuaded to cooperate and support a National Legal Service then that might be an indication that adequate resources have been devoted to it and that it is proceeding on the correct principles.

Suggested Answer

A National Legal Service would be a service provided and funded by the State with employed lawyers. This would be available to litigants in civil proceedings and defendants in criminal proceedings. The State already spends large amounts of public funds on the legal aid system and therfore this money could be diverted to a National Legal Service so that this may be a financially viable proposition. Therefore it has to be considered whether, in principle, this is a wise idea.

As part of the considerations of principle one has to consider whether there is a need for a National Legal Service in the same way that there is a need for a National Health Service. Health services are something that we all need at some stage in our lives and many people cannot carry on life without medical help. But a large percentage of the population can avoid the need to use legal services. In terms of priorities the quality of legal services to a deprived community is not as important to them as the quality of health care. However, some form of basic legal services is a human right and therefore society should try to make such services available. If the private legal profession has failed adequately to provide such services then a properly organised National Legal Service becomes an objective that should be achieved and on that basis is akin to a National Health Service. Further if legal assistance can be elevated to the same status as a health service then it is arguable that just as you would not want to ration a health service then the availability of legal services should not be rationed.

The existing arrangements for publicly funded legal services involve legally aided services carried out by lawyers in private practice, Citizens' Advice Bureaux in various parts of the country, and law centres. Law centres are mainly found in London and other major cities.

It has to be considered whether a National Legal Service would be better than these existing arrangements.

Arguments against Implementation

It has been argued that a Crown Defence Service for criminal matters which would be the criminal part of the National Legal Service might be under–resourced and therefore not provide an adequate service because the best legal brains would not be attracted to it and proper defence preparation could not be carried out. However, it is argued that it cannot be any worse than the currently underfunded legal aid system. With the existing legal aid system not all lawyers take on legal aid cases which restricts the choice that poorer defendants have. Further it would be very difficult for any government to justify giving more funding to a Crown Prosecution Service than to a Crown Defence Service. In fact it would be easier to argue that a similar level of funding should be given to both organisations.

With a private-practice solution there is a tendency for some lawyers to spin out a case and make it as complicated as possible. In a National Legal Service with regulated fees and better methods of dispute resolution, unnecessary expense would be avoided.

Arguments in Favour of Implementation

One of the main problems with the existing public-sector arrangements for funding law centres and Citizens' Advice Bureaux is that the government will not provide comprehensive national funding and takes the attitude that the primary providers should be local communities through local government arrangements. That has meant that not all areas of the country are served and the level of services varies greatly. There has been a contraction of the availability of these services. There is no obligation on solicitors to undertake legal aid work so again some areas are served better than others. A proper national funding would mean that a minimum standard of service would be available for all areas.

It is arguable that the service could look at ways of taking preventive measures, i.e., it does not have to wait for individuals to come forward if it can recognise a legal problem that affects the community at large.

Suggested Principles upon which a National Legal Service should be Based

The Birkenhead resource unit has suggested that a National Legal Service should be based on the following principles:

(a)   That legal services for the community should be redefined as legal care with the aim of improving the quality of people's lives.

(b)   That there must be a balance struck between individual case work and strategic and preventative work so that the service delivered has the maximum effect for the good of the community generally.

(c)   That a legal service should be seen as part of a comprehensive approach to improving the quality of lives of local people and, therefore, there must be clear linkage with strategies on, and services for, health care, education, income maximisation and local economic development, and most importantly urban regeneration issues.

(d)   That there should be a commitment to education and training for the community.

Conclusion

All governments since 1945 have accepted that there should be public funding of legal services for those who cannot afford them. When the legal aid scheme was originally set up it was intended to cover at least 70 per cent of the population. Law centres and Citizens' Advice Bureaux developed to deal with problems at a lower level that are serious to the individual who needs counselling and some form of advice but would not think that a solicitor would or could deal with it. Therefore the question is whether a National Legal Service is the best way to deliver publicly funded legal services.

It may be arguable that civil legal aid is not a human right but there is a general acknowledgment that the right to a defence counsel in criminal proceedings is a human right and that for there to be a fair trial and a fair sentencing process there needs to be legal representation. The government is a signatory to the European Convention on Human Rights and one of the human rights that is protected is the right to a fair trial. Therefore adequate legal representation for criminal proceedings is something that all British governments must maintain.

It should be seriously considered whether a public defence system would be better than the existing arrangements.

5 The Judiciary

INTRODUCTION

The questions in this chapter will start by looking at the constitutional role of the judges, and then consider specific concepts such as independence, neutrality and impartiality. It is then necessary to consider the appointment process, security of tenure, training, discipline and removal and how these contribute to ensuring independence, neutrality and impartiality.

Questions about the judiciary are topical because of the following factors:

(a)   A Law Society campaign for changes in the appointment process because they argue that it has the effect of discriminating against solicitors.

(b)   The judges' role in the series of cases known as the miscarriage of justice cases.

(c)   The adverse publicity and perception that in some cases too low sentences concerning rape and sexual offences have been passed and also the reaction to what have been considered to be insensitive remarks about how a woman might be able to recover from such an ordeal.

(d)   Campaigns from civil liberty groups such as Liberty and Charter 88 who believe that the judiciary must be reformed if a Bill of Rights is introduced in the UK. They question whether the general composition of the judiciary from a narrow social background would be able to give the necessary weight to social and political factors central to making human rights decisions. Reform of the judiciary is part of the agenda for constitutional reform. These bodies also highlight the inadequacies of judicial training.

(e)   A belief that the appointment process is too secretive, lacks proper accountability and has inadequate checks and balances.

(f)   If Lord Woolf's report *Access to Justice* is fully implemented then it will mean a new role for the judiciary at trial level which will require greater training so that they can become effective 'trial managers'.

QUESTION 1

Evaluate the effectiveness of constitutional rules which seek to maintain the independence and impartiality of the judiciary. To what extent do these constitutional arrangements achieve this?

Commentary

Certain laws and conventions have developed to try to ensure that the judiciary can function independently and impartially. These rules have to be analysed and assessed to see whether they really do achieve independence and impartiality. There are also some arrangements which on the face of it may create an impression that independence could potentially be compromised, such as the position of the Lord Chancellor, and they need to be assessed.

Suggested Answer

The constitutional role of the judges is to interpret and enforce the law.

There may be disputes between individuals and companies against the government or government departments or emanations of the State. Criminal proceedings are proceedings by the State against the individual. In those situations it has to be considered whether the judges would put themselves on the side of the State, giving preference to its view when there is a conflict of evidence or when decisions have to be made about whether an individual has enforceable rights.

The concepts of independence and impartiality are constitutional principles that should be upheld.

Independence

Independence means independence from the government, and from improper pressure by the executive, by litigants or by particular pressure groups.

Independence means far more than immunity from interference. It means that judges are free to bring their sense of values to bear in considering legislation and do not simply reflect the values of the government.

Independence and impartiality are connected concepts because independence is a precondition of impartiality and of fair trials. It is a necessary part of the constitutional doctrine of separation of powers which enables the courts to check the activities of the other branches of government.

Another way of expressing what the independence of the judiciary means is that the judiciary should not become a mouthpiece of the executive. The courts are there to protect the rights of the individual against the State by ensuring that executive powers are lawfully exercised.

Discussion of the independence of the judiciary must consider how wide that concept is. Does judicial independence imply that the executive must have no voice or a muted voice in the appointment or promotion of judges? Some would consider that the concept of judicial independence would require freedom from political influence in the appointment of judges. Does the independence of the judiciary mean that neither the executive nor the legislature shall be competent to remove judges? If the executive and legislature are to have no role in appointments and dismissal then arrangements in the United Kingdom must be altered. To what extent should judges remain aloof from public feeling and public opinion on an issue before them? Judicial independence should not have to mean that judges have to be isolated from society.

Impartiality

Judges must not only be impartial but they must appear to be impartial as well.

Impartiality means that a fair hearing would be given listening carefully to all sides and reaching a result which is not influenced by the fact that one of the parties is the goverment or an organ of the government. Impartiality means not merely an absence of personal bias or prejudice in the judge but also the exclusion of irrelevant considerations such as the judge's political or religious views. Individual litigants expect to be heard fully and fairly and to receive justice. Essentially, this view is based on judicial neutrality which is regarded as more than impartiality between the parties. It means, also, that the judge should not consider matters which go beyond those necessary for the decision in the instant case.

Security of Tenure

The independence of the judiciary was confirmed in the Act of Settlement 1700. This laid down a rule (now in the Supreme Court Act 1981) that judges held office during good behaviour but were subject to a power of removal by an address of both Houses of Parliament. This procedure is designed to build and protect the independence of the judiciary by making it difficult to remove the senior judges. This would remove them from the danger of being subjected to political pressure. However, it has been thought that the safety of this procedure really has been because governments have not been prepared to use it, i.e., because of the self-restraint of politicians and the circumspection of the judges.

Judicial Salaries

Salaries are an aspect of security of tenure. The Act of Settlement 1700 provided that judicial salaries should be 'ascertained and established'. This was interpreted as requiring that judicial salaries should be fixed by Act of Parliament and not left to the discretion of the executive. To deal with this aspect judicial salaries are charged on the Consolidated Fund, which means that the authority for payment is permanent and does not have to be reviewed by parliament each year. Judicial salaries can be increased but not reduced.

Rules Concerning Politics

Judges should be independent of politics. This is supported by a convention that judges do not take part in party politics and that their political sympathies must not affect their judgment. By statute, superior and circuit judges cannot be Members of Parliament. Law Lords are not supposed to take part in political debates in the House of Lords though they do speak on law reform. There can be a fine line between the two in practice. Another convention is that members of the House of Commons do not attack a judge on a personal basis, except by moving an address for the judge's removal. But criticism can be directed at the legal principle laid down in a case or concerning the sentence.

Judicial Immunity

The judges' independence of thought and opinion is also protected by the doctrine of judicial immunity.

The purpose of judicial immunity is so that a judge can work in complete independence and freedom from fear (*Sirros* v *Moore* [1975] QB 118). A judge may not be sued in a civil action for things said or acts done in the exercise of the judicial office, provided they are within jurisdiction or honestly believed to be so. This even includes malicious and defamatory statements provided they are made within jurisdiction (*Anderson* v *Gorrie* [1895] 1 QB 668).

Role of the Prime Minister in the Appointment Process

All senior judicial appointments are made on the advice of the Prime Minister, but it can be argued that appointments should be made by an independent body such as a Judicial Appointments Board.

Role of the Lord Chancellor

The Lord Chancellor is not just head of the judiciary. He is at the same time a member of the Cabinet and Speaker in the House of Lords. He is a political appointee in the sense that he holds office only during the office of the government that appointed him. When there is a change of government, he will resign with that government. The Lord Chancellor is supposedly guided by the convention that his political activities must be kept completely apart from the judicial responsibilities of his office. But as a member of the Cabinet he is a member of the executive which means that he is bound by the doctrine of collective responsibiity. That means in reality that his first loyalty is to the government and its policy, i.e., he has to support government policy publicly and cannot speak out against it publicly. For example, if government policy is that public spending, including legal aid, has to be cut then he has to support that.

The Lord Chancellor's role has been criticised because it has been felt that it is not possible for him to reconcile his potentially conflicting roles. In the 1980s the Bar brought judicial review proceedings against the Lord Chancellor concerning the low rates of remuneration for barristers who were undertaking legal aid work.

During those proceedings it was realised that the barristers arguing this case were appearing in front of judges who included those appointed by the Lord Chancellor and those whose prospects of promotion depended on him. In those circumstances it was realised that a more independent method of appointment would give the appearance and reality of greater independence. In the 1990s the Lord Chancellor introduced more reforms concerning legal aid which were highly criticised and the Law Society commenced judicial review proceedings.

These events highlight that the Lord Chancellor's political, legislative and judicial roles do not sit easily together and emphasise the lack of separation of powers.

There is a view by the Law Society and some political parties that the political functions of the Lord Chancellor should be removed, given to a Cabinet

Minister who would be a member of the House of Commons and head of a new Ministry of Justice.

Conclusion

Some constitutional rules attempt to secure the independence and impartiality of the judiciary but may be undermined by other rules.

The rules that govern the independence and impartiality of the judges have to be the product of a balance. The judges must be free to decide cases without fear but there are certain matters that are not inconsistent with the independence of the judiciary. It has been argued by Geoffrey Robertson QC (*Freedom, the Individual and the Law* (Penguin)) that judicial independence is not inconsistent with procedures to investigate complaints by citizens against the judiciary, or with a rule that any judge who commits an imprisonable offence automatically loses office, or with the monitoring of performance and standards by a judicial commission. Nor is it incompatible with rules for regular medical and psychiatric examinations.

QUESTION 2

The idea of a judge being impartial needs more consideration than it is often given. General outlook, unspoken values, and mental habits can have just as much influence without being so noticeable. Consider the criticisms that have been made about their general outlook and values and assess its impact on the quality of judicial decision making and the public perception in general.

Commentary

This question is a deeper consideration of the theme set out in question 1. In question 1 the meaning of independence and impartiality was explored with specific reference to the actual constitutional rules and arrangements that either contribute to independence and impartiality or actually weaken it. Here we are looking at the more subtle ways that impartiality and independence can be affected such as the background and upbringing of the types of persons appointed as judges.

There are at least three different levels of lack of independence of the judiciary:

(a)   Crude lack of independence. This would be where a Minister or his representative informed the judges of the result wanted by the government.

This is something that it is said does not happen in most countries. Another form of crude lack of independence is bribery from one or more of the parties for a particular result.

(b) Subtle lack of independence. This is where judges are appointed who are in the same mould as those who are in power in the government, i.e., the establishment. These judges will know what to do and their decisions reflect establishment thinking and values. This can potentially happen in many countries which is why the UK and the USA have the additional safeguard of trial by jury. If subtle lack of independence exists then there is no need to resort to crude lack of independence because the same result can be achieved.

(c) Restrictions on the judges' powers. The independence of judges is compromised if they cannot exercise much freedom of decision-making, for example, where there are mandatory sentences for criminal offences, which removes the judges' discretion concerning sentencing.

Suggested Answer

Impartiality means that judges should not be prejudiced or biased in their judging but should decide cases before them in a fair manner. A judge who feels that he or she would be biased or has an interest in the outcome of a particular case should excuse him- or herself from hearing that case.

A litigant may object to the involvement of a particular judge on the ground that previous judgments cause the litigant to doubt whether the judge would decide the case impartially. In 1978 Lord Denning MR accepted such an application in a case concerning the Church of Scientology where counsel was of the view that Lord Denning's previous judgments showed doubt whether he would hear the case impartially (*Ex parte Church of Scientology of California* (1978) *The Times*, 21 February 1978).

In 1984 there was an application that Lord Lane CJ should not hear a case concerning the use of roadblocks by the police to stop striking miners reaching picket lines. Counsel for the miners argued that Lord Lane would be influenced by comments he had made, adverse to the miners' legal claim to conduct such activities in an earlier case. Lord Lane was of the view that he would be able to hear the case fairly but that he was prepared to accept counsel's request. The case was then heard and decided in favour of the police by the other two judges (*Moss* v *McLachlan* [1985] IRLR 76).

Unspoken Values

Judges have what might be described as 'unspoken' values which are the result of their upbringing, the social circle that they move in and the working environment. The inherent values include the fact that the judges are predominantly from the middle class or the upper middle class, and were educated at public schools and the older universities such as Cambridge or Oxford (known for short as Oxbridge). Alternatively they come from grammar school but were able to win a place at Oxford or Cambridge as Lord Denning did. Lord Denning was known not to support trade unions against employers or fellow employees who did not want to belong to a trade union.

Even if someone comes from a modest background and does not go through public school or Oxbridge, by the time they are appointed a judge at 40 to 50 years of age, they have become middle class and have imbibed the values of this class. The judges are still predominantly from members of the Bar. As the Bar has been dominated by the middle class and upper middle class then if you want to be accepted in such a setting you take on the values of those who are in the majority. In general the study and practice of law would either reinforce existing values already had as part of the middle class or, if not, it is likely that these would be developed because of peer pressure within the legal profession, especially at the Bar.

The Bar itself, in a book entitled *The Quality of Justice* (London: Butterworths, 1989) which set out the Bar's response to the Green Papers proposing changes to the legal profession, argued that the ethos of the Bar produces the type of the judiciary that we have. The Bar describes the training the barristers go through, with their entire professional life in the courts, in strong competition with other barristers, regularly cross-examining witnesses, weighing and summarising evidence, expounding the law and testing their arguments in Socratic dialogue with the judges. The Bar acknowledges that barristers go through a social conditioning process. The Bar argues that this produces high-quality judges with strength and independence but it does have the effect of producing a judiciary with broadly similar attitudes.

Rodney Bickerstaffe, a trade union leader, in an interview in the *Legal Executive* magazine in September 1992, criticised the judges. His view is that there has been a failure of government, courts and the legal profession to protect adequately the rights of workers and people. He is of the view that the interpretation of employment law has been interpreted in a restrictive manner which has tilted the balance in favour of employers. Bickerstaffe attacked the divided legal profession arguing that it creates counsel who are too isolated and remote from the clients they represent and who eventually become remote and isolated judges.

Lord Denning has stated that on appointment a judge puts to one side his politics and prejudices. This is likely to be wishful thinking. Professor Griffith in his book *The Politics of the Judiciary*, 4th ed. (London: Fontana Press, 1991) makes it very clear that he does not believe that complete neutrality can be achieved in practice. He argues that judges are part of the authority of the State and will tend to make conservative decisions which support the existing order as they see it. Professor Griffith argues that the courts' approach to the police has been an example of this.

Attitudes to the Police

It can be argued that Lord Denning took a pro-police view in his judicial career, for example, when the Birmingham six wanted to sue the police for damages for injuries that they alleged they had suffered Lord Denning stopped the action because he stated that if the men's allegations of violence and threats were true then it would mean that the confessions would be erroneous and that this would be such an appalling vista that the case could not proceed. The trial judge in the Birmingham six case had stated that these allegations were an implied slur on the police. In 1987 when the Birmingham six case was referred back to the Court of Appeal it was felt that Lord Lane's attitude during the appeal showed that he had prejudged the matter and had refused to believe the allegations that were made about the police conduct. After the final Birmingham six appeal succeeded in 1991 Lord Denning stated that he had not realised that the police could have behaved in this manner.

Some judges have shown that they have supported proposals for change that the police have wanted. For example, the police have been in favour of pre-trial defence disclosure and limitations on the right to silence. In *R v Alladice* (1988) 87 Cr App R 380, Lord Lane CJ made it clear that the defence should not be able to take the prosecution by surprise at trial. In 1994 Lord Taylor of Gosforth CJ said that he was in favour of limitations on the right to silence.

Attitudes to Women

Another area of concern by women's groups has been the judges' attitudes towards women. The judges are predominantly male and the allegation that has been made is that there is a subtle bias against women in the law and how it operates in practice. The solution proposed by women's groups is that more women should be appointed as judges.

Insensitive remarks made by judges about women has led to concern, i.e., a feeling that ageing male judges often seem to take sexual assaults against women less seriously than the rest of society. For example, a woman hitch-hiker who was raped was described as being guilty of 'a great deal of contributory negligence' by Judge Bertrand Richards in 1982. A former High Court judge, Sir Melford Stevenson supported Richards's view and stated that any girl hitching was 'asking for it'. Mr Justice Leonard, in 1987, described the trauma suffered by the victim of a rape, who was 21 and a virgin at the time of the rape, as 'not so very great'. Her response to that was that the trial judge did not have a clue as to what she had been feeling. In 1990 Judge Raymond Dean told a jury concerning a rape that when a woman says no, she does not always mean no and that men cannot turn their emotions on and off like a tap as some women can. The jurors acquitted the accused. These comments provoked an outcry over the judge's attitudes.

New Approach in Recent Years

In 1992 the presidents of the criminal and civil divisions of the Court of Appeal, Lord Lane CJ and Lord Donaldson of Lymington MR, retired and were replaced by Lord Taylor of Gosforth CJ and Sir Thomas Bingham MR. There was a feeling that a new type of judge had been promoted to these positions which would lead to a new approach.

Lord Taylor spoke of his new approach in the Dimbleby Lecture in 1992 entitled 'The Judiciary in the Nineties'. He considered whether the judiciary are remote and stuffy. He was of the view that a certain degree of detachment is inevitable if judges are to maintain their independence and be seen to do so, for example, 'It would be unwise for a judge to frequent a pub beside the court where he might run into one of the lawyers or witnesses in this current or next case'.

Lord Taylor went on to consider whether the judges are establishment minded and so biased in favour of the prosecution in criminal cases and of the government in civil cases. He argued that the fact that judges were called upon to chair inquiries was evidence of independence and an ability to be objective. Judges have chaired inquiries into industrial relations disputes, public disorder, corruption in public life, standards in public life, football ground disasters, child abuse, the working of the prison system, prison riots, the collapse of

BCCI, and the arms for Iraq scandal. Lord Taylor chaired the inquiry into the Hillsborough football disaster. He said that the criticism that he received was that he had been too hard on the police. He was of the view that judicial bias towards the establishment does not bear examination. Since the 1980s the biggest development in the law has been judicial review. This is the procedure which enables an aggrieved citizen to have the court rule whether government, central or local, or public bodies have exceeded their powers, acted unreasonably or short-circuited necessary safeguards. Not all of the actions have been successful but many times ordinary citizens have been successful against government departments, the actions of Ministers, housing authorities, education authorities, prison authorities, and immigration authorities.

The development of judicial review does not suggest a pro-establishment position. In fact the government became so concerned about judicial review in the mid 1980s that a government booklet was produced entitled *The Judge over your Shoulder* to inform civil servants about the perils of judicial review and to advise them how to make decisions which would not be subject to a successful judicial review application.

By 1995 the government was questioning whether the judges' approach to judicial review had gone too far and it was being reported in the press that Ministers had been angered both by the growing number of successful challenges to their actions through judicial review and by judges pushing at the boundaries of judicial review so as to widen its scope.

Conclusion

The question indicates that the judges' outlook, values and thinking have not been so noticeable. That is not true. Professor Griffith has noticed and forcefully written about it. Other organisations such as Charter 88, Justice and Liberty have also noticed and made recommendations for reform which would attempt to tackle this problem.

The effect of the debate on this has been to put pressure on the Lord Chancellor's Department to show that there is an attempt to appoint persons who would be considered to be more liberal in thought. An example of this was the appointment in 1992 of Stephen Sedley QC, a member of Liberty, to the High Court bench. There is also a view that the House of Lords has been transformed by an influx of radical independent-minded judges which has led to a liberalism and a judicial bravery that has never been seen before the 1990s. These developments are an indication that if liberal-minded persons are appointed then that will translate into liberal-minded decisions. Again proving the theory that judges cannot totally put to one side their inherent views.

Further in the light of all these developments since 1992 it is now arguable that Professor Griffith's views have to be re-evaluated. He wrote that the judges were substantially pro-establishment. However, by 1995 the government certainly does not have that view of the judiciary. It has been reported in the press that they regard the judges as interfering busybodies in the way they overturn Ministerial decisions by judicial review.

QUESTION 3

The lay magistracy and the jury are not the only amateurs in the criminal justice system. The judges also have an inadequate professional knowledge of the criminal law and the practicalities of the trial process. Further appeals lie to a court which may be composed of judges who have not specialised in criminal law. Discuss.

Commentary

This question requries careful interpretation because it can be mistaken as being concerned with the lay magistracy and the jury. This question requires a consideration of the qualifications, experience and training that those judges dealing with the criminal law would have both for general criminal work and also specialised aspects of the criminal law such as long fraud cases. The central theme of the question is that judges in criminal trials might have little experience of the criminal law.

Suggested Answer

The theme of the question is that judges who preside over criminal trials are not specifically skilled to deal with criminal trials and criminal law. The question criticises both trial judges and appellate judges.

Selection

Trial judges include, in the Crown Court, assistant recorders, recorders, circuit judges and High Court judges. In making appointments, the Lord Chancellor looks for character, temperament and intellectual ability. A newly appointed judge will sit part-time, generally as an assistant recorder or recorder in the Crown Court. Some very high flyers may sit as a deputy High Court judge in the High Court dealing with civil matters. If they fulfil this part-time capacity in a satisfactory manner for usually at least three years they would then be invited to accept a full-time appointment.

It is possible for judges to be selected to sit in the Crown Court who have not practised in the criminal field. The last time that they studied criminal law would have been at university! Therefore there will be judges who will not be familiar with criminal trials, criminal law and criminal procedure. There is always criminal law and procedure in the books and there is the actual practice and experience that goes on in the criminal courts, which would be what the question describes as the practicalities of the criminal process. The practicalities would be the experience of both defending and prosecuting, of dealing with other participants in the criminal process including judges, the prosecution, the police and defendants. Also watching the reaction of victims and their responses to the criminal process.

The Court of Appeal is divided into two divisions, civil and criminal. It is the Criminal Division that hears criminal appeals from the Crown Court. The judges in the Criminal Division are Lords Justices of Appeal and also High Court judges on secondment. The Criminal Justice and Public Order Act 1994 permits circuit judges also to be seconded. Appeals in the Court of Appeal are heard by benches of three and generally there is someone on the bench who has experience of criminal trials and criminal appeals.

The final appeal court is the House of Lords which hears appeals from the Court of Appeal on matters of public importance. There are 11 Law Lords and an appeal would generally be heard by five, amongst whom there would be judges who have experience of hearing criminal appeals.

Training

Newly appointed assistant recorders and recorders undergo about four days of training.

In addition to the classroom training the newly appointed judge would sit for at least 10 days with a more experienced judge. At present there is some continuing education known as 'refreshers', generally for a day. There is no specific training when there is promotion to a higher court.

This amount of training has been considered to be inadequate especially where somebody who has been appointed as a judge has not spent much time practising as a lawyer in the field of criminal law. The organisation, Justice, believes that the training should be for three to six months and should be more substantial covering criminal law, criminal evidence, criminology, penology, forensic science (which is often a weak area amongst lawyers), psychology, policing techniques, sociology, meeting with victims, dealing with specialised areas such as complex fraud, and learning about complicated accounts and financial transactions such as reading a balance sheet. Racial awareness training is necessary and this has been introduced with effect from 1994. Further when a Bill of Rights is enacted or the European Convention on Human Rights becomes part of UK law then training in this area will be necessary. There also needs to be greater comprehensive practical training which would include mock trials, sentencing exercises, and practice in addressing a jury.

In addition, there needs to be comprehensive, regular compulsory continuing education.

The Royal Commission on Criminal Justice recommended a substantial increase in resources for judicial training. The Royal Commission made it very clear that this was necessary in the interests of justice which requires competent judges who are fully abreast of the latest developments in law and practice. Such training would be cost-effective because better trained judges may be able to ensure that trials can be kept to manageable lengths and be better able to explain and understand complex points. Mistakes avoided at first instance prevent time wasted on appeal.

The Royal Commission on Criminal Justice also recommended monitoring of the performance of judges during training and that there should be an effective formal system of performance appraisal.

Ability to Perform the Judicial Function

Generally most judges perform their functions adequately and professionally. If they do make mistakes with regard to the law then these can be corrected on appeal. Misdirecting on the law might suggest a lack of ability with the criminal law and therefore a need for more training in this area. The Judicial Studies Board has produced a set of draft directions for trial judges to follow so that misdirections would not be so frequent.

An area where judges have been criticised for their lack of professional approach concerns the passing of too lenient sentences and insensitive comments made to victims. The Criminal Justice Act 1988, s. 36, now allows the Attorney-General to appeal where a judge has passed a too lenient sentence. However, this is generally only done in cases where there has been a public outcry. Pressure for such a change had been building up ever since a judge in the early 1980s had fined a man for raping a hitchhiker because he took the view that the woman had been contributorily negligent.

Appellate Judges

The attitude of some appellate judges has been criticised in that it has been felt that they were unable to believe that the police could be lying. When Lord Lane CJ heard the 1987 appeal of the Birmingham six he refused to believe the stories of violence against the six by the police and he said during the hearing that the longer the appeal went on the more convinced he was that the men were rightly convicted. This was believed to be a prejudgment of the appeal, which was dismissed. The trial judge in the Birmingham six case had stated that he disbelieved the six's accusation that they had been beaten up by the police and told the jury that this was a slur on the police. The six were convicted. Later the men brought a civil action claiming damages for injuries received as a result of the police beating. Lord Denning MR stopped the action on the basis that if the men's allegations of threats and violence by the police were true then the confessions would be erroneous and that would be such an appalling vista that the men's actions should not proceed. Ultimately the criminal conviction was referred back to the Court of Appeal for a second time. New evidence cast doubt on the reliability of the men's convictions which were quashed.

House of Errors

Lord Donaldson of Lymington has described the House of Lords as a House of Errors because of its misinterpretation of the criminal law in the case of *Anderton v Ryan* [1985] AC 560. The reality of the matter was that the House of Lords did not want a housewife to be convicted of attempting to handle stolen goods because the video recorder that she bought was not stolen when she thought it was stolen. A year later in *R v Shivpuri* [1987] AC 1 the House of Lords realised that they had not properly interpreted the Criminal Attempts Act 1981.

These cases raise the question whether, as so few criminal cases do go up to the House of Lords, the Law Lords have enough day-to-day contact with the criminal law for their decisions to be sound in principle. On average the House of Lords hears only about 30 criminal appeals per year. Certainly the House of Lords' approach concerning duress has been criticised as illogical. The House of Lords will not allow duress to be a defence to murder (*R* v *Howe* [1987] AC 417) or attempted murder *R* v *Gotts* [1992] 2 AC 412). However, duress can be argued as a defence for all other offences.

Conclusion

The statement made in the question is correct to the extent that judges may be appointed to hear criminal cases when they have not practised criminal law during their practice as lawyers. They do receive some training but it is not comprehensive, for example, it does not cover criminal law and procedure because the judge is expected to know that already. It does cover matters which a person would not have experience in, such as instructing a jury. Therefore some judges in terms of experience and expertise may initially be considered to be amateurs. However, they are scrutinised for their competence when undertaking a part-time appointment. As full-time judges they would rapidly develop experience and expertise. This would transform them into professionals in the true sense of the word.

With regard to the appellate courts, whilst it is true that some of the judges may not have a strong criminal background it should be remembered that they sit with other judges who do. In that way experience and expertise are developed by all the judges. With regard to a case such as *Anderton* v *Ryan* the criticism is not a lack of experience with criminal law but a question of statutory interpretation. Alternatively it might be argued that in *Anderton* v *Ryan* their lordships placed too much emphasis on the effect on the housewife and not enough on the conduct that the prosecution was seeking to deter, namely, the attempted handling of stolen goods.

QUESTION 4

Should a career judiciary be adopted? Or alternatively a mixture of a career judiciary supplemented by recruitment from the Bar and the solicitors' profession?

Commentary

There has been severe criticism of the inadequacy of training for judges. Another criticism has been that the judiciary comes from a too narrow background with glaring deficiencies concerning the small proportion of women and people from the ethnic minorities. Tony Holland, former president of the Law Society, predicted that something radical would have to be done if substantially more women and ethnic minorities are not recruited to the bench. In countries where there are career judiciaries they do not experience these problems. Therefore the career judiciary might be the radical way forward or at least there is a need for a mixture.

Suggested Answer

In a career judiciary most judges spend their entire working lives as judges after appropriate training. They follow a judicial career and are promoted to higher judicial office according to the career structure of the judiciary without ever having been engaged in the day-to-day practice of the law. Career judges are mainly found in the European legal systems. Whereas in the common law systems the judiciary is largely, but not entirely, chosen from among practising lawyers and there are no career judges.

Drawbacks of a Career Judiciary

The main benefit of the system of appointing lawyers from the most senior practitioners is that both the judiciary and the legal profession have the benefits of the best legal brains. The Bar attracts people of quality and these persons later become judges. In a career system lawyers have to choose whether to be judges or not, which might lead to those who cannot make it at the Bar trying to join the career judiciary service.

The cost of introducing such a system would be significant and it is this factor that will keep serious consideration of this idea from being developed.

There are some areas of the law where no amount of teaching and training would be a substitute for actual experience and expertise developed in practice. This is especially true in construction, shipping and corporate law.

Separating practitioners and judiciary would require people to make a choice early in their careers when they may not fully know what they want to do and there may be a high attrition rate when new appointees realise that they would rather practise or do something else. If the judge's qualification is useful or prestigious to have then some may obtain the qualification, be judges for a while and then leave for practice or industry. There is currently a rule that judges cannot return to practice and it would be difficult to maintain such a rule if judges are appointed in their mid 20s.

In European legal systems there are no lay magistrates and so the newly qualified judges can start at this level and work up. European judges generally sit in benches of three so that the newly qualified judge can sit with more experienced ones. A career judiciary would mean that the lay magistracy would have to be abolished. Abolition would be strongly opposed by the Magistrates' Association. Even if this problem could be resolved one wonders whether high-flyers would be attracted to magistrates' court work or small claims work.

Reasons Why a Career Judiciary should be Considered

There is frustration from women, ethnic minorities and solicitors that they are not being appointed to the judiciary in sufficient numbers. The London Solicitors Litigation Association believes that the solution to this is a career judiciary. Such a judicial branch could have a recognised training programme available to all suitably qualified entrants, with a defined examination or appraisal system, a clearly understood appointments system and a progressive career structure through the judicial hierarchy.

A radical approach is needed because there is going to be continued pressure upon the legal system arising from the fact that the pool of qualified lawyers from which the judiciary is drawn is so small.

The reason why solicitors are not available for judicial work in the same numbers as barristers is because of the different structure of the solicitors' branch of the profession. Barristers are essentially sole practitioners and can more easily devote time to initial part-time judicial appointments. In contrast solicitors who practise in partnership are often severely constrained from accepting part-time judicial appointments because of their partnership obligations. A solicitor cannot, within the discharge of partnership responsibilities, take significant time off at levels of remuneration far below what he or she would normally be expected to contribute.

A career judiciary may be the only way to ensure that judges are not culled almost exclusively from the ranks of the Bar but come from all walks of life.

Another benefit of a career judiciary would be to ensure that younger people come to the judiciary so as to get away from the feeling that becoming a judge is something that is done when people are coming up to retiring age.

Need for Properly Structured Training

It continues to be realised that there is a need for greater training which would include further refresher training. A career judiciary would institutionalise that need because proper training programmes would have to be provided and that would have the general knock-on effect of greater resources having to be devoted for this purpose. In European jurisdictions new career judges undergo about four to six years of full-time training. Experienced practitioners who are appointed in these jurisdictions undergo about one year of training.

If judicial case management becomes a reality there will be a need for a proper training programme to teach the judges how to carry out this function adequately. Sir Jack Jacob QC (1986 Hamlyn lectures 'The Fabric of English Civil Justice') has stated that there would be a need for a career judiciary if the UK ever adopted the inquisitorial system. A feature of the inquisitorial system is judicial case management. Presumably the reason for his view was that this would be the only way to introduce a properly structured training programme and also to entice people with the hope that they would be promoted to higher judicial posts in the long run.

Conclusion

A career judiciary with some entry from the legal profession could be the best of both worlds. It would not be wise to rely only on a career judiciary but it looks increasingly that it is no longer satisfactory to rely on legal profession entry only because of the segments of society it effectively excludes. Another reason why there should be a mixture is because real high-flyers may only be attracted later on with a judicial post and so these persons should not be ruled out with a rigid career judiciary structure. Flexibility should be important but it does have the danger that the career judiciary might be seen as second best and that perception should be avoided where possible with proper career development programmes and real promotion prospects being available.

6 Magistrates

INTRODUCTION

The magistracy is comprised of a small number of professional magistrates called stipendiary magistrates and a large number of non-professionals known as lay magistrates or justices of the peace. The magistrates are found in the magistrates' courts. Lay magistrates are also found in the Crown Court where two to four may sit with a professional judge deciding appeals from magistrates' courts. The questions below will explore the role of magistrates in the criminal justice system of which they are the mainstay. One point to be considered is the trend to increase the workload and responsibility of the magistrates at the expense of the jury. This trend has not been acceptable to certain civil liberty groups as they are not prepared to accept that magistrates embody the lay principle in the same way that they consider the jury does. It could be argued that one reason for highlighting criticisms about magistrates is to try to create a 'bad press' so that the government has to think very carefully before increasing their jurisdiction and role in the criminal justice system any further.

One of the areas of criticism concerns arguments about inadequacies of training and the need for a national minimum standard. A response to this came in 1996 with the production of a training video which covers: (i) Bail, (ii) Sentencing, (iii) Mode of Trial, (iv) Trial.

There is written back up to the video, which is presented as part of a teaching seminar. The video covers the style and type of hearing that magistrates can expect.

QUESTION 1

Most persons' contact with the criminal justice system will be with the conduct of cases in the magistrates' courts. Therefore their opinion of the quality of the law and how confident they are in the system will be shaped by this experience. To what extent does the way in which magistrates are selected, trained and supervised build confidence in the system?

Commentary

The quality of the justice in the magistrates' courts is continually being assessed and debated. It is a source of continual amazement that part-time amateurs who have not had a full legal training and professional legal background actually undertake this function. This question will consider whether this type of background can make for good-quality decision-making and inspire confidence as a result.

Suggested Answer

Most defendants who are charged with a criminal offence will have come in contact with the magistrates' courts, which deal with the following:

(a) Deciding whether the police should be permitted an extension of detention in custody beyond 36 hours for further questioning before charge (Police and Criminal Evidence Act 1984, s. 43).

(b) Bail applications.

(c) Determining mode of trial.

(d) Trial.

(e) Conduct of youth courts where most offences concerning youths are tried.

Therefore most impressions concerning the fairness of the criminal justice system will be formed in the magistrates' courts.

Confidence

The word 'confidence' connotes trust in an institution. Lord Hailsham has said that what people want is injustice, meaning that if they are charged with a criminal offence but are guilty of it they want to be acquitted. Therefore it has to be realised that if more defendants want to have trial by jury it can imply a lack of trust in the magistrates' courts but it can also mean that accused persons want to try a system where there is a greater chance of acquittal. That could mean that the jury is more prepared to give benefit of the doubt to defendants or that the magistrates are less gullible. Studies have shown that professional judges have a higher conviction rate than juries.

As about 98 per cent of all criminal cases are dealt with by the magistrates' courts, if those courts are deficient in any way then that would affect public confidence in the criminal justice system generally.

Selection and Appointment

There are no minimum educational qualifications or any other formal qualifications for appointment as a lay magistrate. But there are some disqualifications, covering bankrupts, persons with a conviction for a serious crime or a series of minor crimes, members of the armed forces, the police and their spouses, traffic wardens, or anyone with impaired hearing, sight or other serious infirmity. MPs, Parliamentary candidates and full-time election agents cannot be lay magistrates in their own constituencies but they can sit in others. Anyone who has an occupation that would conflict or be incompatible with the duties of a magistrate is also disqualified. Anyone married to a person with a conflicting or incompatible occupation would also similarly be disqualified.

Persons chosen to be lay magistrates must exhibit certain qualities, namely, character, integrity and understanding and must be generally recognised as having these qualities by those among whom they live and work.

Because the magistracy is a part-time volunteer organisation, only those who have the time can undertake this function. Magistrates' courts sit in office hours during the day. Therefore only people who are at work and can get permission for time off work or those who are not working can be lay magistrates. The minimum level of commitment needed is to be able to attend 26 ½ days a year. Therefore the bench is dominated by middle-class persons. Attempts have been made to do something about this such as advertising campaigns but they have not made a substantial improvement in terms of attracting more working-class persons to sit on the bench because employers are reluctant to allow such persons time off from work. Further there is also a view that peer pressure amongst the working class is to regard magistrates as part of the establishment so that there would be some suspicion of a fellow worker who became a magistrate.

There is also concern about the selection process. Approximately 2,000 new lay magistrates are appointed each year. They are appointed by the Lord Chancellor on the recommendation of about 100 advisory committees throughout England and Wales. The composition of these committees is dominated by serving magistrates and it is felt that these committees will tend to pick persons like themselves, and serving magistrates are themselves predominantly middle class.

Training

Magistrates generally are not already legally qualified on appointment. They will have many different backgrounds not connected with law. They will either be not working or have work that permits them to undertake this function. Thus they need some specific training to equip them for the task of judging cases. They will be considering both the law and facts in each case. Magistrates generally sit in benches of three and so a newly appointed magistrate would sit with more experienced magistrates and gain experience in that manner. The most senior magistrate of the three in terms of suitability and ability would be the chairman and would have attended further training for chairmen. The magistrates are assisted by a justices' clerk who can advise them about law and procedure. The justices' clerk also assists in training magistrates.

Since the 1960s there has been compulsory training for magistrates. This training will not convert lay magistrates into qualified lawyers. It can be described as 'basic' and is not even remotely close to a professional training. This training can be divided into three stages: training before appointment, training during the first year of appointment and then refresher training in subsequent years.

Training before appointment includes being informed about the obligations of upholding the judicial oath and human awareness training to promote awareness of differences of ethnic, religious and cultural practices and habits. The nature of the criminal process, the court structure and the adversarial nature of proceedings will also be taught. Such training may be given in about three hours. There will also be practical exercises, called participatory decision-making exercises. These would be completed in about six hours. The exercises are designed to develop decision-making skills in dealing with bail applications, reaching a verdict and passing sentence. In addition a newly appointed magistrate must spend about another six hours observing proceedings in a court other than the one in which he or she will sit.

After the induction stage of training has been completed the magistrate is entitled to sit with more experienced magistrates.

During the first year of appointment a lay magistrate must visit a local prison, a young offender institution and the probation service. There is further training amounting to about 12 hours.

In the second and third years there are four hours of training.

There is further training in subsequent years amounting to 12 hours every three years. This amount of training can be considered to be inadequate especially when one considers that even solicitors are now expected to undertake yearly compulsory continuing education to keep up to date. Further there is concern that some magistrates are not bothering to attend some of these courses.

Additional training is necessary for lay magistrates who are to sit in the youth court and the family panels.

This training can be described as very thin. But the safeguards in the system are that:

(a)   The people chosen are supposed to have already shown in their careers or other public service, such as work in the community, the qualities that will make them suitable and able to judge and sentence others.

(b)   Initially they sit with more experienced lay magistrates who can guide them, and there are annual courses that will give more training.

(c)   The justices' clerk can help to fill in the gaps of their legal knowledge and experience.

Supervision

The dictionary definition of supervision is to oversee, direct, inspect and control.

The justices' clerk's function is not to do any of those things but to advise on the law and procedure should the lay magistrates need assistance. There is, however, the supervisory jurisdiction of the Queen's Bench Divisional Court and both the defence and prosecution have the right to ask the magistrates to state a case should they believe that the magistrates have not applied the law correctly or have exceeded their jurisdiction.

The Lord Chancellor could remove a magistrate for misconduct. The power to do this is contained in the Justices of the Peace Act 1979, s. 6. No specific grounds justifying a removal are set out in the Act. However, in practice a justice would only be removed for good cause. Resignation is required if a magistrate is not able to sit for the minimum amount of time each year or has ceased to live within 15 miles of the local commission area in which he or she sits. With regard to misbehaviour the overriding consideration that has to be considered is that public confidence in the administration of justice must be preserved. Thus magistrates have resigned following conviction of an offence, though minor motoring offences will lead to a reprimand rather than suspension or removal. The local advisory committee generally will consider whether there is any substance to allegations of incapacity or misbehaviour and if they conclude that the lay magistrate should be removed then that is reported to the Lord Chancellor's Department. If the lay magistrate does not accept the committee's findings then there is a further consideration by the Secretary of Commissions.

Conclusion

The question rightly points out that most persons' contact with the criminal justice system is the magistrates' court. However, the real feeling that is generated about the magistrates is that there are higher conviction rates in the magistrates' courts than in the Crown Court, in fact nearly double.

If the magistrates' courts continue to be composed of lay and professional magistrates there will always be higher conviction rates because of the supervisory jurisdiction of the Queen's Bench Divisional Court. Therefore the ordinary person will always be attracted to a court where acquittal rates are higher. Thus no amount of adequate selection, training and supervision will change peoples' minds in this respect.

The higher conviction rates do not necessarily show that the magistrates are more conviction minded but that the higher acquittals in the Crown Court are due to other reasons. One reason could be numerical. At the Crown Court, the prosecution have to convince at least 10 out of 12 jurors that the defendant is guilty. In the magistrates' court only two out of the three lay magistrates have to be convinced or, if the trial is by stipendiary magistrate, only one. Another reason could be that the magistrates are predominantly persons from the middle

class who may have more respect for and trust in the police than juries do.
Further most juries come fresh to criminal cases whereas magistrates hear
hundreds of cases each year and may become 'case-hardened'. Magistrates
may hear inadmissible evidence which would be kept from jurors because
questions of admissibility are decided by the magistrates themselves whereas
in the Crown Court such questions are dealt with by the trial judge in the
absence of the jury. Even if the magistrates rule some evidence to be
inadmissible they have still heard it and may be subconsciously affected by
having heard it.

QUESTION 2

Is there any justification for keeping lay magistrates other than their cheapness?

Commentary

The reason why it is crucially important to make the lay magistracy more
representative is because if it is not then that undermines one of the main
reasons for having the lay magistracy. Although an advantage of the lay
magistracy is cheapness it is becoming increasingly questioned whether the lay
magistracy is really as cheap as was thought. If the lay magistracy can never
be made to reflect a cross-section of the public, is not really as cheap as it was
thought to be and is not as good at decision-making as the professionals then
there are no main benefits of having a lay magistracy and it really should give
way to a professional system of magistrates.

Suggested Answer

The question suggests that cheapness is one of the main attractions of the lay
magistracy. However, the government has always stated that the main reason
for the lay magistracy is that it represents the lay principle. The only problem
with that is that there are serious problems that are not easy to overcome in
ensuring that the lay magistracy is truly representative of the local population
where they sit.

Lay Principle

The lay principle is about providing a common-sense view by ordinary persons.
The purpose of the criminal law is to set minimum standards of conduct and it
should be lay persons who decide what those standards should be. Lay
magistrates can provide more effective feedback to the government concerning

unpopular legislation than professional magistrates. Examples of unpopular legislation include lay magistrates refusing to enforce the community charge (poll tax) and resigning in consequence of it. Also a number of lay magistrates resigned after the Criminal Justice Act 1991 required them not to take into account the previous convictions of an accused when sentencing and required them to calculate fines on a formula of units that took into account the accused's earnings which meant that for some very minor offences very high fines were imposed. The general dissatisfaction concerning these provisions led to the government repealing them in the Criminal Justice Act 1993. It has been alleged that some lay magistrates are hostile to the Criminal Justice and Public Order Act 1994 and are looking very carefully at the cases being brought under the Act concerning public order offences. The penalties imposed so far (up to November 1995) do suggest an unwillingness to use it to the full. The maximum fine available under the Act is £2,500 but the maximum fine so far imposed is £200. Offenders may be jailed for three months but nobody has yet been jailed (*The Economist*, 11 November 1995).

Input of Women

So far a significant number of women have been attracted to the lay magistracy. Approximately 42 per cent of lay magistrates are women.

The professional judiciary by contrast has not been able to achieve such a constitution and therefore female presence in the lay magistracy on this scale makes a significant contribution to the female presence in the criminal justice system.

Local Knowledge

Lay magistrates are appointed to serve within the locality and have to live within 15 miles of the commission area for which they are appointed. Such a rule would not be feasible with professional magistrates. The benefit of this rule is that local conditions can be taken into account by magistrates when hearing cases.

Ability to Undertake the Function Expected of Lay Magistrates

Most cases coming before the magistrates are straightforward. They are able to handle these cases and it is not necessary for more expensive professional magistrates to be employed.

The lay magistracy developed in the thirteenth century and it is necessary to consider whether what was appropriate for those times is still appropriate for an industrialised country after vast technological changes and increasing complexities of law and of life.

Most of the time lay magistrates deal with straightforward cases concerning theft, minor violence and road traffic. About half the workload concerns traffic offences. Most motoring offences are straightforward because they are strict-liability offences — all that has to be ascertained is whether the act has been committed, for example, was the accused exceeding the speed limit or driving with alcohol beyond the permitted amount? The magistrates do not have to consider why the person was in that situation. In reality the offences that the magistrates are dealing with today are no more complex than centuries ago. If they were acceptable and adequate in the past then it can be argued that the lay magistrates are not out of place today.

Conclusion

There are advantages to the lay magistracy other than cheapness. It may be that the reasons other than cheapness will continue to ensure that a lay magistracy is still relevant. Accordingly the argument that the lay magistrates are not as cheap as it has always been thought and that stipendiary magistrates may be much more efficient is not necessarily a reason for replacing lay magistrates with stipendiaries.

7 Trial by Jury

INTRODUCTION

Trial by jury is a controversial institution. Can a jury really understand and follow the issues in a criminal trial? Would trial by professional judges be cheaper and quicker? These are the types of issues that can form the basis of questions.

Questions may also require a consideration of the alternatives should the jury be abolished. If the jury is abolished then more attention will be focused on judges and their ability to identify guilt and innocence. It will also lead to a greater examination of whether the judiciary is really independent of the government.

There have been some changes in trial by jury recently. The Criminal Justice and Public Order Act 1994 has disqualified persons on bail in criminal proceedings from sitting as jurors in criminal proceedings (s. 40), introduced a new procedure for determining the capacity of a disabled person to act effectively as a juror (s. 41) and excused from jury service practising members of religious societies or orders with tenets or beliefs which are incompatible with jury service (s. 42). Section 46 makes criminal damage up to a value of £5,000 a summary-only offence. This is an increase from £2,000. Section 51 creates two new offences of intimidating a juror and harming or threatening to harm a juror.

One of the Royal Commission on Criminal Justice's recommendations was that a person accused of a triable-either-way offence would no longer have a right to elect trial on indictment. The venue for the trial would be settled by agreement between the prosecution and defence and in cases where there was a disagreement the magistrates would decide. This proposal was criticised by many including the Lord Chief Justice. Critics pointed out that the category of triable-either-way offences originally contained offences that were previously triable on indictment only. So when the triable-either-way concept was introduced by the Criminal Law Act 1977 no rights of trial by jury were being taken away because the defendant had a right of election. In fact choice was being increased. If this right to choose by the defendant is taken away then effectively this has reduced the right to trial by jury. A consultation document was issued in 1995, entitled *Mode of Trial* (Cm 2908), seeking views on whether trial for minor thefts should become summary only.

QUESTION 1

Juries will never be representative of the public conscience because of the current methods of selection, exclusion, exemption and challenge procedures. Discuss.

Commentary

The question offers the opportunity to indicate knowledge of the current basis of jury selection and the current methods permitted to structure composition, for example, the grounds for eligibility, excuse, dismissal, challenge for cause and stand-by. It should also be considered whether juries are intended to be 'representative' of the public conscience and whether they could ever be, or indeed whether it is possible to describe and define what the public conscience could be. This would include a consideration of public opinion.

Suggested Answer

Selection

The principle is that selection should be random. Effect is given to this principle by drawing the jury from persons aged 18 to 70 on the electoral rolls for the catchment area of the Crown Court in a random way (Juries Act 1974, s. 1 as amended by the Criminal Justice Act 1988, s. 119).

It was Lord Denning MR in his judgment in *R* v *Sheffield Crown Court, ex parte Brownlow* [1980] QB 530 who said:

> Our philosophy is that the jury should be selected at random — from a panel of persons who are nominated at random. We believe that 12 persons selected at random are likely to be a cross-section of the people as a whole — and thus represent the view of the common man.

The view of the common man would be the public conscience.

The problem with random selection is that it sometimes produces an unrepresentative jury. Even Lord Denning in the *Brownlow* case stated that it would be 'likely'. The unrepresentative nature of the jury is most glaringly seen when a non-white person faces an all-white jury. Unfortunately under the present law there is nothing that the trial judge can do to redress this imbalance (*R* v *Ford* [1989] QB 868).

The Royal Commission on Criminal Justice recommended that the trial judge should have the power in exceptional circumstances to allow up to three persons from ethnic minorities with at least one or more persons from the same ethnic minority as the defendant to sit on the jury. However, the Royal Commission was not prepared to recommend that the judge should have a general power to allow this in every case but only in exceptional cases. The Royal Commission gave some examples, namely, that a black defendant charged with burglary would be unlikely to succeed in such an application but that black people accused of violence against a member of an extremist organisation who they said were making racial taunts against them and their friends might well succeed.

R v *Ford* concerned motoring offences. Ford faced an all-white jury. The defence had wanted a multiracial jury. The trial judge had refused this. Ford was convicted and appealed arguing that the trial judge had been wrong to deny the request for a multiracial jury. The Court of Appeal upheld the principle of random selection as the best way of achieving fairness and therefore held that the trial judge had no power to empanel a multiracial jury and no power to discharge a competent juror so as to obtain a multiracial jury. The reason for this is because the law provides that fairness is achieved by the principle of random selection which is the whole essence of the jury system. Lord Lane CJ was also concerned that the mere fact that a jury member is of a particular race or holds a particular religious belief cannot be made the basis for a challenge for cause on the grounds of bias or any other grounds. A judge who removed a juror on either of these grounds would be assuming bias where none was proved. This approach is unjustified in law and is also seriously derogatory of the members of the jury who have to give way for a non-white person. Lord Lane was of the view that the courts could not allow the development of a principle that there should be a racially balanced jury because if that principle were to apply it would mean that there was a view that jurors of a particular racial origin or holding particular religious beliefs are incapable of giving an impartial verdict in accordance with the evidence. Only Parliament should decide this.

Where a black defendant is tried by an all-white jury then this is arguably not trial by jury of his or her peers, or by a jury which is representative of a cross-section of the public conscience.

The Royal Commission on Criminal Justice realised that more should be done to ensure that the jury is randomly selected by ensuring that electoral rolls are comprehensive and include everybody who ought to be included. This is necessary for achieving the purpose of securing jurors who are properly representative of the general population and represent the public conscience.

Exclusion

Certain categories of persons are excluded, namely, those connected with the administration of justice and also the clergy. The reasons for excluding such persons is because they may have an undue influence on the rest of the jurors and also may have particular knowledge of court procedures, for example, knowing that if a *voir dire* (trial within a trial) has been called then admissibility of evidence is being tested. However, the Royal Commission on Criminal Justice could not understand why clergy and members of religious orders should not be eligible for jury service and recommended that they should be eligible. This recommendation has not been implemented.

The other persons who are excluded are those who have been convicted and sentenced to certain periods of imprisonment. The Juries Act 1974 lays down that any person who has at any time been sentenced in the UK either to imprisonment for life, or for a term of five years or more, or has been detained during Her Majesty's pleasure shall be disqualified from jury service. Any person who, within the last 10 years, has served any part of a sentence of three months or more will also be disqualified. The Juries Disqualification Act 1984 has extended the scope of this last basis of disqualification by providing that anyone who within 10 years has served any custodial sentence or received a suspended sentence or been made subject to a community service order will be disqualified. It also disqualifies for five years anyone placed on probation.

The Royal Commission on Criminal Justice recognised that research might reveal that persons with criminal convictions did not adversely affect the decision-making process. Nevertheless it recommended that persons on bail awaiting trial should be disqualified from serving on a jury. This change was introduced by the Criminal Justice and Public Order Act 1994.

Probably the greatest departure from a true cross-section of the public is caused by the excusal as of right of certain categories and discretionary excusal of others. Those who are excused as of right include members of both Houses of Parliament, full-time members of the armed forces and persons in the medical and nursing professions. However, the discretionary excusals can dramatically distort the representativeness of the jury because people can be excused if they have an acceptable excuse. Further there is a *Practice Direction (Jury Service: Excusal)* [1988] 1 WLR 1162 which states that such applications must be dealt with sensitively and sympathetically. Pressing work commitments and having to look after small children may be excuses that will be accepted. Persons with responsible jobs may be more likely to make a successful application for excusal. These persons are likely to be from the middle class.

In an article in *The Times*, 13 June 1995, Hedley Goldberg reported that she had spoken to a spokesman for the Lord Chancellor's Department about who serves on juries. The spokesman had stated that any jury may consist of teachers, builders, company chairmen, stockbrokers and the unemployed. There would have to be a genuine reason for excusal and generally individuals will not be excused because of their job or even if they are self-employed. However, for a trial that is scheduled to last six months applications for excusal will be dealt with more leniently than for shorter trials. Hedley Goldberg came to the view that the main criteria employed in selecting the jury for the trial of two sons of the media tycoon, Robert Maxwell, in 1995 was whether the prospective jurors were available for such a trial. Professor Michael Zander has described this type of jury as 'self-selecting'. Thus for long trials it can be argued that random selection is distorted and the jury contains those who are available which may not be a true cross-section of society and therefore does not truly represent the public conscience. Professor Zander was of the view that such juries contain a disproportionate number of housewives and unemployed persons.

The Royal Commission on Criminal Justice was concerned about the effect excusals have on composition and recommended that alternative dates should be given to prospective jurors so that they could serve at a time that will be more convenient to them or which gives them an adequate opportunity to rearrange their affairs in order to leave time for the jury service to be performed.

Challenge

A juror may be challenged for cause if there is a reason why the juror should not serve. This procedure is rarely used because the defence generally do not know anything about the prospective jurors other than their names and addresses. Thus challenge for cause does not affect the jury's representation of the public conscience. The prosecution's right of stand-by is also rarely used. Guidelines have been issued by the Attorney-General (*Practice Note (Jury: Stand by: Jury Checks)* [1988] 3 All ER 1086), which state that the right must not be used so as to influence the overall composition of a jury or with a view to a tactical advantage. The right of stand-by may be used where a jury panel has been vetted or a juror is manifestly unsuitable and the defence agree that he or she should be excluded. An example is when it is known that a juror is illiterate. Vetting a jury would take place where the case concerns national security and part of the evidence is likely to be heard in camera or where the case concerns terrorism. It would be sensible to exclude a juror who might reveal information that was given in camera. In both security and terrorist cases there is a danger that a juror's political beliefs would be so biased as to go beyond reflecting the broad spectrum of views and interests in the community to reflect the extreme views of sectarian interest or a pressure group to a degree which might interfere with fair assessment of the facts of the case or lead the juror to exert improper pressure on fellow jurors. Jury vetting has been criticised as distorting the composition of the jury. However, Clive Ponting in an official secrets trial in 1985 faced a vetted jury but was acquitted.

Conclusion

The question states that juries will never be representative of the public conscience because of the way in which they are selected and also because of those who are excluded or excused from jury service. The position of the non-white defendant facing an all-white jury clearly shows that random selection does not always produce a cross-section of the public conscience. The exclusion and exemption categories also deplete the number of persons who make up the public conscience. It is hard to believe that the jury *never* represents the public conscience though there has been no research into how frequently the jury does or does not accurately represent a broad spectrum of the public conscience.

QUESTION 2

Random selection of juries produces injustice, and it is time to accept that an impartial jury is more important. Discuss.

Commentary

The problem with random selection is that it involves no consideration of the actual suitability of the individual jurors to try the particular case before them or whether the composition gives the appearance of fairness to the accused. This question requires a consideration of how to reconcile randomness with these equally important considerations. The Roskill Committee's recommendations should be mentioned concerning complex fraud cases. The Roskill Committee was of the view that random selection was not suitable for complex fraud trials because of the complexity of the evidence, the length of trials and the limits of comprehension. These views should be balanced against the arguments in favour of random selection, for example, the absence of evidence that the current system is unworkable, public confidence in the present system, and the value of the current jury system for judging dishonesty.

Suggested Answer

This question concerns two competing principles: first random selection and what it is hoped to achieve, secondly impartiality. Random selection is supposed to achieve a jury representative of a cross-section of the population and in that way should achieve fairness.

It would be useful to consider the American position. The sixth amendment to the constitution of the United States of America lays down the right to an impartial jury. To ensure that this right has real meaning there is a pre-trial jury selection process. This process allows the defence and prosecution lawyers to question prospective jurors to assess whether they are impartial. The benefit of this process is that the general intellectual abilities of the jury can be tested which would seem to be the best way of achieving a fairer composition of the jury. Leaving the achievement of a fair jury to chance cannot be a firm foundation for a jury system. However, with this method of jury selection the defence try to achieve a pro-defence jury likely to acquit and it can be argued that this is an abuse. American lawyers talk about the dream jury which is a jury that is likely to acquit. During the American jury selection process the defence may have psychiatrists in attendance to assess prejudice from beliefs or background or even body language. It is up to the prosecution to try to counter-balance this by putting forward arguments as to why a juror is suitable. The trial judge makes the final decision. However, this can be a time-consuming process. For example, the jury selection in the O.J. Simpson case took about one month.

It is doubtful that jury selection would ever be introduced into the UK, not even in modified form. The concerns would be the costs and potential abuse by defence lawyers contriving to achieve a jury composition more likely to acquit. The defence used to be able to challenge up to three jurors without giving a reason. It was alleged that in the Cyprus spy trial 1985, the defence lawyers agreed to pool their peremptory challenges to attempt to produce a jury that was young, working-class, anti-establishment, unpatriotic, mainly male. In the end an unusually young jury was achieved with an average age of about 24. All the seven defendants were acquitted. It was felt that this persuaded the government to abolish the right of peremptory challenge which was eventually done by the Criminal Justice Act 1988.

The experience with the peremptory challenge shows that there is no way that a British government would permit American-style jury selection.

Abolition of the peremptory challenge has caused one unexpected side effect. It was used to help ensure that some non-whites could be on a jury trying a non-white person. This has caused practical problems because some blacks do not like facing an all-white jury. It might be insulting to say that some of the whites would not be impartial but it is more important to deal with how the blacks feel and what they perceive. There are also problems when the victim is black. An example is the trial in 1995 of the police officers charged with the manslaughter of black Joy Gardner. She had been an illegal immigrant. The police officers had been assigned to arrest her so that she could be deported. Restraints were put on her that caused her to suffocate. The police officers were acquitted by an all-white jury. There was a feeling in the black community that justice was not achieved here, and this was articulated by Bernie Grant MP as reported in *The Times*, 15 June 1995. He felt that the system had let black people down and that in future people might find other ways of expressing their anger, though he urged protesters to use democratic means and not to resort to violence.

This problem is not going to go away and has to be addressed. The Court of Appeal left the state of the law in a very unsatisfactory position as a result of *R* v *Ford* [1989] QB 868 in which the view taken was that randomness produces fairness and impartiality. However, Profesor J. Gobert has stated that 'a randomly selected jury is not an end in itself; it is only a means to an end. The end is the empanelling of an impartial jury' ('The peremptory challenge — an obituary' [1989] Crim LR 528).

Fairness and impartiality are aspects of justice and there is an important maxim that not only should justice be done but it should be seen to be done. When a non-white faces an all-white jury the appearance of justice is missing. In August 1995 a survey was published in the *Daily Express* which showed that two thirds of Britons were racist to some extent and half thought non-whites should be given money to help them return to their country of origin. If the white population as a whole think this way then a jury could have a majority of white persons on it who think this way. In those circumstances a non-white is justified in taking a view that he might not have a white jury that will approach matters with an open mind.

The Royal Commission on Criminal Justice recommended that up to three jurors from ethnic minorities should be permitted to sit on a jury in exceptional cases. This recommendation has not been accepted yet and the Lord Chief Justice has spoken out against such a change on the basis that it affects the principle of random selection. However, only one of the three jurors might come from the same ethnic minority as the defendant. It should also be remembered that there is a false assumption here that people from other ethnic minorities are not racist against blacks. They can be. Further there is the majority verdict. Even if there are two blacks on the jury they cannot stop a majority verdict being returned as a verdict of guilty can be on the basis of 10 in favour of conviction and two against. Some blacks who see only one or two blacks on a jury consider this composition to be tokenism. It is ironic that two reforms introduced for other reasons have caused such tension concerning the ethnic minorities. The majority verdict was introduced because there was a fear that juries could be nobbled by organised crime. The peremptory challenge was abolished because it was felt that it was being abused.

This is a clear area where the principle of an impartial jury should dominate over the principle of randomness and it should be realised that randomness in this area is not working. If the American legal system is compared, in the O.J. Simpson trial the jury at the end consisted of nine blacks, two whites and one Hispanic. There were 10 women. Eight of the women were black, the other two were white. One of the two men was black and the other was Hispanic. Such a jury composition would never have been achieved in the UK under the existing rules.

There is so much secrecy surrounding the jury that it is not possible to assess whether the UK method of random selection regularly produces injustice or not. The Contempt of Court Act 1981, s. 8, makes it a criminal offence to interview a juror about, or for a juror to disclose, what went on in the process of reaching a verdict. The right to know a juror's occupation was abolished in 1973 by Lord Chancellor Hailsham because of allegations that defence counsel at trials arising from industrial picketing were using the information to work out whether a juror might be a member of a trade union.

In *R* v *Pennington* (1985) 81 Cr App R 217 the Court of Appeal refused to quash the conviction of a striking miner for picketing offences after it was discovered that one of the jurors had been a strike-breaking miner. It can be argued that this was very unfair because the defendant was being tried by a foe and it would be highly likely that this person would not be impartial. It can be argued that this kind of problem will happen again and again until the right to know the occupations of members of the jury panel is restored to the defence. This would involve giving priority to the principle of an impartial jury over random selection.

One benefit of requiring an impartial jury is that the search for such a jury would include an assessment of the intellectual abilities of potential jurors. One fundamental concern about trial by jury in the UK is whether the jury can really understand and follow the issues in cases such as complex fraud cases. A jury selection process that tested intellectual abilities would contribute to an impartial and fair trial process. In the UK there is concern about achieving fair trials in complex fraud cases.

Conclusion

There is evidence that random selection might in certain situations produce injustice or potential injustice, e.g., a black defendant facing an all-white jury or an *R* v *Pennington* situation. Whilst random selection is a good underlying principle it has to be recognised that achieving an impartial jury is more important and therefore steps need to be taken to achieve that, for example, ensuring that the principle of a multiracial jury takes precedence and that the defence should know about the occupations of the potential jurors.

Full-blown American jury selection will never be accepted in the UK but some modified form should be considered, such as greater use of detailed question- naires or only the judge being able to ask the questions.

QUESTION 3

Is there any sense in carrying on relying on common men and women to follow evidence and reach the right verdict in trials of serious criminal offences?

Commentary

The first point to note is that it has to be decided which court the question refers to. The key words are 'common' and 'serious'. The jury deals with serious criminal offences. This question concerns justifying the use of juries in criminal trials.

After the key words have been identified the overall theme should be considered. A key word that has to be given consideration in this question is 'sense' which means having or showing sound judgment. But sense from which point of view? It is necessary to consider the smooth administration of justice, the government's point of view, the politician's point of view, the point of view of public confidence, the civil liberties point of view and the defence's point of view.

Suggested Answer

Ordinary people are chosen at random to sit on a jury to try cases that are to be heard in the Crown Court. All trials in the Crown Court are by judge and jury. There has been a concern that the jury may not be able to appreciate fully the evidence being dealt with at trial and then give the necessary weight to this evidence so as to reach a correct decision.

It is very difficult to know precisely whether juries are capable of following evidence and are able to reach a correct verdict because juries do not give reasons for their decisions. They simply enter a verdict of guilty or not guilty.

Section 8 of the Contempt of Court Act 1981 has the effect of making research into the jury illegal if it asks jurors questions about how they arrived at their verdict. Nevertheless it can be considered whether in principle it makes sense that ordinary people should continue with such a role.

Lack of Qualifications

No minimum educational qualifications are imposed for sitting on a jury. Therefore there is no guarantee that all jurors would have an adequate educational level to be able to follow the evidence. Professor Hogan said that the jury carries out a professional task, i.e., a function that needs trained persons, and therefore an untrained jury is not fitted for its task.

Fraud Trials

Fraud trials deal with evidence that is acknowledged to be complex concerning complicated financial transactions and tracing of money, requiring a knowledge of accounts and accounting practices, and share dealings and complicated methods of cheating. Yet the jurors in these trials will not have been subject to even a literacy test. Fraud trials often take three to six months and so only those who are available for such time will sit. This means that such juries will be dominated by the unemployed, the retired, those who do not work or those who have jobs they will not miss or be missed from, such as manual workers. These will be the type of persons who are not used to sitting still trying to absorb a mass of detail.

A majority of the committee on Fraud Trials (the Roskill Committee), which reported in 1986, were in favour of abolition of trial by jury and for it to be replaced by a Fraud Trials Tribunal comprising a judge and two lay expert assessors chosen for their familiarity with business and financial matters. The majority of the Roskill Committee came to their views relying heavily on 'the promptings of common sense'.

This recommendation has not been accepted by the government. The Royal Commission on Criminal Justice would not make any recommendations in the absence of proper research. However, it can be argued that if juror comprehension is a problem than it is a strong argument for abolition.

In the absence of comprehensive research, scrutiny is made of individual cases. Each time there is a long highly publicised case, the media and even academics write that not only are the defendants on trial but so is the jury. One such case where these comments were made was *R* v *O'Callaghan* (1995). This concerned a mortgage fraud and the trial lasted for six months before the defence barristers submitted that the jurors should be discharged because the huge amount of evidence had become 'oppressive and unmanageable'. The trial judge discharged the jury because he decided that he could not know whether the jury would understand enough evidence to be capable of reaching a proper verdict. There was also an allegation that two of the jurors had been playing what the English call noughts and crosses (tick-tack-toe). The trial was scheduled to last another four months and the judge thought that his summing up to the jury would have taken at least 14 working days. The judge doubted whether the jury would be able to comprehend or remember much of the evidence by the time they retired. In effect he ruled that the evidence was too difficult for the jury.

Following this case it might be thought that there is no point bringing alleged fraudsters to trial if the evidence is too tough for the average juror to understand.

It is not just fraud cases that have caused concern. For example, in 1994 there was a murder case that raised doubts concerning the behaviour of some members of the jury. This was *R* v *Young* [1995] QB 324. Young was on trial for the murder of two victims, a husband and wife. The jury retired to consider their verdict and adjourned to a hotel for the night. While in the hotel four of the jurors purported to make contact with one of the victims using a makeshift ouija board. The message they heard was, 'vote guilty tomorrow'. This was discussed at breakfast with other jurors who had not been present at the ouija board session. The Court of Appeal held that there was a material irregularity in the trial, quashed the conviction and ordered a retrial. Their lordships concluded that there was a real danger that what had happened during that 'misguided' ouija session might have influenced some of the jurors and might have prejudiced the verdict. The Court of Appeal was of the view that the four jurors had taken this ouija board session seriously and that it was not a game. At the retrial, Young was again convicted.

Conclusion

From a rational point of view it would seem to be far more sensible if criminal trials were heard only by professional judges who would be trained to follow evidence and reach correct decisions. However, a lot of emotion surrounds the jury and it would seem that this emotion centres on the jury being a safeguard of our liberties rather than whether the jury can follow the evidence and reach a correct decision in every single case.

QUESTION 4

Support for trial by jury is based on strong emotions and sentimental views about the value of the jury. This is not going to be dented one way or another by research evidence which shows the unreliability of the jury's verdict. Discuss.

Commentary

This question requires a consideration of why there is so much support for the jury, and whether there are strong rational reasons for the continuance of the jury which override any adverse research showing the unreliability of jury verdicts. However, to date there has not been any such conclusive research.

The question also requires an exploration of what supporters of juries call jury equity, i.e., justice and fairness to the individual defendant even though that might not be consistent with the strict letter of the law. Critics would describe verdicts arrived at in that way as perverse because they ignore judicial directions on the law or are, to judicial thinking, irrational.

Suggested Answer

The *Report of the Committee on Defamation*, chaired by Mr Justice Faulks (Cmnd 5909, 1975), considering trial by civil jury for defamation actions, identified the value of the criminal jury: 'We believe that much of the support for jury trials [in defamation cases] is emotional, and derives from the undoubted value of juries in serious *criminal* cases, where they stand between the prosecuting authority and the citizen'.

There is one thing that a jury can do which a professional judge cannot do and that is to perform 'jury equity'. This is where the jury is able to consider the greater justice of the situation and acquit. This function has been a feature of the criminal jury for centuries, e.g., the eighteenth-century sheep-stealing cases where juries refused to convict sheep stealers because they thought the penalty, death by hanging, was too harsh.

There have been some trials in the 1980s and early 1990s where it can be speculated that juries acquitted because they disapproved of the police or prosecution techniques or the motives behind the prosecutions. These cases include the trial of Clive Ponting, the Cyprus spy trial and the trial of Randle and Pottle. These cases show that politically motivated prosecutions do take place and that the Faulks Committee's statement is correct.

Ponting was charged under s. 2 of the Official Secrets Act 1911. He was a civil servant and was accused of disclosing 'official information' without authority to an unauthorised person. The 'official information' was two documents about events during the Falklands War and the sinking of the Argentinian cruiser *General Belgrano* in May 1982. These documents had been sent to a member of Parliament and passed to a select committee of the House of Commons where they had played an essential part in its enquiries into the sinking. Ponting had confessed to what he had done. His defence was that the Act says that it is not an offence for a person to communicate a document if it is his duty to do so 'in the interest of the State'. Ponting argued that it was in the interest of the State for Parliament to be told that it was being misled by the government. The trial judge directed the jury that 'the interest of the State' meant the interest of the government. The jury acquitted.

Lord Devlin was of the view that the Ponting case could be explained on the basis that the jury acquitted because '. . . they had refused to apply an Act of Parliament widely regarded as unfair and oppressive, but left unrepealed so as to satisfy Whitehall [civil service] bureaucrats' ((1991) 107 LQR 398 at p. 404).

It has been argued that the acquittal in the Cyprus spy trial was because the prosecution case had been undermined and the defendants had been subject to heavy-handed treatment when in custody.

Seven young servicemen were charged under s. 1 of the Official Secrets Act 1911 with passing secrets to Russian agents. The case against them was that they had been blackmailed into spying after being lured in homosexual orgies. However, these allegations seemed inconsistent with what was known about the servicemen. They had all worked in secret communications monitoring bases at Ayios Nikolaos in Cyprus. The prosecution relied on detailed confessions said to have been made to the RAF police. The defendants' case was that these confessions had been forced out of them.

Randle and Pottle were charged with assisting the escape from prison of George Blake who had been sentenced to 42 years in prison in 1961 for spying. It has since been alleged by Tom Bower in *The Perfect English Spy* (1995) that the Prime Minister at that time, Macmillan, had insisted that Blake should be given a long period of imprisonment. Randle and Pottle represented themselves at trial. They argued that they should be acquitted because it was over 25 years since they had committed the crime and the case had been dragged up after pressure from MPs. They also argued a 'necessity defence', that they had a right to break the law because they were freeing George Blake from the 'cruel and unusual punishment' of a 42-year sentence which endangered his life. The judge directed the jury that this defence did not apply. The defendants asked the jury to act like juries in the eighteenth-century sheep-stealing cases and the Clive Ponting case where juries had acquitted even though the evidence indicated guilt. They also pointed out that at Ponting's trial the judge had told the jury that Ponting had no defence in law yet the jury acquitted.

The jury acquitted Randle and Pottle and it can be argued that this verdict was made in defiance of the law. It may be that the 25-year delay in prosecution was the most important factor in the jury's decision.

Existing Research Findings

Critics of the jury usually say that:

    (a)   juries acquit in too many cases, and

    (b)   juries cannot really understand and follow the evidence.

The Oxford Penal Research Unit has carried out two studies. The first, published as *The Jury at Work* in 1972, concerned 115 jury acquittals from a sample of 475 defendants. The conclusions were that most of the acquittals were attributable to the failure of the prosecution to present a good enough case rather than any perverseness on the part of the jury. The second study, published as *The Shadow Jury at Work* in 1974, involved the use of shadow juries to listen to real cases and then comparing their decisions with those of the real juries. There was an agreement rate of 75 per cent.

However, the research of Baldwin and McConville, which was a study of trials in Birmingham, has presented a less favourable view of jury decision-making (*Jury Trials*, 1979). Baldwin and McConville concluded that juries were sometimes too ready to acquit people who appeared to be guilty and to convict people who might be innocent. This view should be counterbalanced with the views of other participants in the Criminal Justice System who Baldwin and McConville interviewed using questionnaires, namely police lawyers and judges. Their views about verdicts were that mostly, the jury had got it right.

Research was also commissioned for the Roskill Committee on Fraud Trials and was undertaken by the Cambridge Applied Psychology Department/Unit (the unit). The unit carried out studies into juror comprehension by using volunteers sitting as mock jurors. They were asked to listen to the judge's one and a half hour summing up in a fraud case and were then asked questions to test their comprehension and recall of the material. The researchers were of the view that people had difficulty in absorbing complex information. However, the research was not like the real thing because no attempt was made to reproduce the conditions of a trial. The research conditions lacked the repetition of material which would happen in a trial. Also the drama and impact of the trial were missing. Further the volunteers did not have an opportunity to pool their collective memories as juries do which would help those who need to be assisted with their memories and understanding.

The Royal Commission on Criminal Justice commissioned research which was conducted by Professor Zander and entitled 'the Crown Court study'. There was a two-week study of all the Crown Court centres in England and Wales in February 1992. Very detailed questionnaires were given to all the main participants — the judge, prosecuting and defence barristers, the defence solicitors, the CPS, the police, the court clerk, the defendants and the 12 members of the jury. The questionnaire for the jury asked questions such as whether they as individuals and the jury as a whole could understand and remember the evidence and the judge's directions on the law. They were also asked whether any members of the jury could not cope because of a lack of ability with English or any other reason. All the other participants in the criminal justice system were asked whether they thought that the evidence was consistent with the verdict. Under 10 per cent of the jurors said that they had difficulty in understanding the evidence. Foremen of the juries reported that over half of their fellow jurors found little difficulty in remembering the evidence. What other participants in the criminal justice system thought of the jury's verdict was as follows. The judges, barristers and defence solicitors said that they had been surprised in about 15 per cent of cases and the CPS and police in about 25 per cent of cases. With regard to acquittals the CPS and police stated that they were surprised at half the acquittals. The judges and the prosecuting barristers said they were surprised at about 25 per cent of acquittals and defence representatives at between 10 and 14 per cent.

Conclusion

The research considered above can all be dismissed as not being conclusive of anything and the way it was carried out flawed. Thus there is an absence of conclusive research showing that jury verdicts are unreliable. However, the question is of the view that if such research existed it would be dismissed by the supporters of trial by jury. This is probably true because of the jury's role as standing between the prosecuting authority and the citizen.

The reason why general opinion supports the concept of the jury is because support is for the institution of the jury and that is considered to be more important than the individual decisions of the jury. The emotion concerns what the actual institution stands for. It is clear from an analysis of the cases that a jury sometimes takes into account different factors in reaching its decision than a professional judge would. However, civil liberty groups argue that it is this ability to look at all the issues before deciding on a verdict which is an essential constitutional safeguard and plays the role of reducing the harshness of the law.

8 The Criminal Justice System: Principles and Failings

INTRODUCTION

This chapter will examine the principles upon which the criminal justice system is based.

The criminal justice system has been under stress because of a series of miscarriages of justice and also because of the continuing need for effective law and order. It could be argued that these cases represent a small minority when compared to all the cases being dealt with before the courts. Even so the effect of the cases was to sow seeds of doubt in the minds of persons that there could be even more miscarriages of justice.

Restoring public confidence was one of the main reasons for the setting up of the Royal Commission on Criminal Justice in 1991. Unfortunately commentators such as Geoffrey Robertson QC and Joshua Rozenberg have been disappointed by the report and said that it may not reduce miscarriages of justice. In fact some of the recommendations would have the effect of increasing the risk of convicting the innocent, for example the recommendations that plea bargaining should be encouraged and that more cases should be heard in the magistrates' courts where there would be less scrutiny and a higher conviction rate.

QUESTION 1

One way of analysing a criminal justice system has been to create two models, namely crime control and due process. Explain how helpful this method of analysis is when considering the objectives of the criminal justice system. To what extent does the English criminal justice system fulfil these objectives?

Commentary

This question requires an analysis of the objectives of the criminal justice system and an assessment of how it meets those objectives.

Suggested Answer

The objectives of the criminal justice system include the following:

(a)   The conviction of the guilty and the acquittal of the innocent. A really effective criminal justice system would be able to identify the innocent at an earlier stage than trial and not proceed with cases against them. However in the event that a case does so proceed the innocent would be acquitted at trial.

(b)   Should an innocent person be convicted the system should have adequate procedures to rectify the mistake.

(c)   In *R* v *Howe* [1987] AC 417, Lord Hailsham of St Marylebone LC stated that the objective of the criminal law is to provide minimum standards of conduct.

(d)   Maintaining the integrity of the system and also maintaining public confidence in the system.

(e)   To prevent and reduce crime, to provide suitable punishments for the guilty and to deter them and others from reoffending.

(f)   The government has stated that all of the above objectives should be achieved as economically, efficiently and effectively as possible.

It has to be realised that there are competing objectives in a legal system. Miscarriages of justice may occur in two ways. One is when the innocent are convicted and this is what is usually understood as a miscarriage of justice. However, it can also mean that the guilty are being acquitted. Whilst it is the civil liberty groups who are vigilant about innocent people being convicted the police are equally concerned that guilty people should not be acquitted. Further the police are concerned about the need to satisfy public opinion who want criminals to be caught, convicted and sentenced in a manner that reflects the crime. The system therefore has to come to a balance to satisfy these conflicting needs.

Crime control and Due Process

Academics study the nature of a criminal justice system and they want to see how the system is standing up to the competing pressures described above. One way that they have approached this analysis is to use two models, one is called crime control and the other is called due process. These models were originally discussed by H. L. Packer in *The Limits of the Criminal Sanction* (Stanford University Press, 1968). They are two separate value systems that compete for priority in the operation of the criminal process.

Crime Control

Crime control values are those that emphasise the repression of criminal conduct. The emphasis is on efficiency and a high rate of detection. The perpetrators of crime should be caught and the criminal process should operate with speed, uniformity, certainty and the finality of conviction. This model prioritises the conviction of the guilty even at the risk of the conviction of some but very few innocents and with the cost of infringing the liberties of the citizen to achieve its goals.

The supporters of 'law and order' would generally be supporters of crime control values. The police and prosecuting authorities generally hold crime control values.

Due Process

The due process model emphasises the need for procedural safeguards. The procedural safeguards may lead to a loss of efficiency in the criminal justice system but this loss of efficiency is the price which must be paid to guarantee the protection of the innocent. Due process values prioritise the acquittal of the innocent, even if risking the frequent acquittal of the guilty, and giving high priority to the protection of civil liberties as an end in itself.

An example of a due process safeguard is jury trial, which is slower, less efficient and more expensive than a single professional judge. The repression of crime would still be a part of due process but it would have to be subject to adequate procedural safeguards which take priority.

The due process model also involves a belief that there should be equality of resources because otherwise defendants would be at a disadvantage. Thus whenever the system gives a theoretical right for a lawyer to advise or represent a client, the due process model insists that substance be given to that right by providing public funds to those who cannot afford the costs of a lawyer.

Shifting the criminal workload down to the magistrates' courts would be an example of the triumph of crime control values over due process because it is more efficient to process offenders through the magistrates' courts and there is a higher conviction rate in these courts.

Value of the Models

One problem is that the two models may be too simplistic. Sometimes it is possible for those proposing reform for crime control to dress it up so that it looks like due process. An example is the abolition, by the Criminal Justice Act 1967, of the requirement that a jury's verdict must be unanimous. The police had wanted this because of jury nobbling (where one or more jurors are bribed or intimidated to reach a certain result). It was also thought that if a jury could not agree because of one person then it was a waste of resources for there to be a retrial. However, in Parliament the arguments were dressed up as the quest for the impartial jury which should not be tampered with in any way. Presenting the change in this way made it more difficult for the civil liberty groups to oppose it.

The two models emphasise different aspects of the criminal justice system. These models are not perfect but they do provide a crude method of assessing in which direction the system is going. The fact that a proposed reform is in the direction of crime control should prompt consideration of the extent to which this affects due process values, whether there are enough safeguards and whether there should be vigorous opposition to the proposed reforms.

Extent to which the English Criminal Justice System Fulfils its Objectives

One of the problems of having competing values is that a due process approach would argue that attention must be given to developing effective procedural safeguards against certain types of evidence and certain types of prosecution behaviour. It is this behaviour that has a proven tendency to cause wrongful convictions. However, if due process safeguards are suggested to deal with this then the proponents of crime control values protest that these safeguards will allow too many criminals to escape conviction. In fact it is the crime control values that are winning in the English criminal justice system.

The miscarriage of justice cases revealed certain problems in the criminal justice system:

(a) Treatment in the police station leading to unreliable confessions. Both the Royal Commission on Criminal Procedure and the Royal Commission on Criminal Justice recommended that the right to silence be continued as a safeguard for vulnerable suspects. However, the crime control proponents' views prevailed because they argued that experienced criminals could exploit the system by keeping silent and avoid conviction. The Criminal Justice and Public Order Act 1994 limited the right to silence. A substantial increase in due process protection would have been if all confession evidence should only be accepted if corroborated. However, the Royal Commission on Criminal Justice was not even prepared to recommend this because it would in effect make it harder to secure convictions.

(b) Unreliable forensic evidence. Nothing substantial has been done about this. The solution is that there need to be laboratories independent of the police and access for the defence to a pool of scientific experts with equivalent experience to those in government service.

(c) Police lying in the witness box. If the safeguards in the police station are improved it becomes more difficult for the police to do this.

(d) A failure by the appeal courts to recognise miscarriages of justice. In recent years there has been a greater realisation concerning this. The Royal Commission on Criminal Justice recommended that the powers of the Court of Appeal to quash convictions should be widened. Better investigation by the Criminal Cases Review Commission may identify unsafe convictions.

(e) Inadequacies of legal aid. There has been no change, in fact it can be argued that this has got worse.

(f) The police and the prosecution not revealing all the evidence that they have in their possession. In the Judith Ward case crucial psychiatric reports on Judith Ward were never revealed by the prosecution. These would have shown that when she confessed she was not in a fit mental state. With regard to one of the Guildford four, evidence of Gerard Conlon's alibi lay unappreciated amongst non-material prosecution papers and was not available at trial. Also material discrediting the most important witness against the Taylor sisters at their trial for murder was withheld by the police and even from the prosecution lawyers. This continues to be an area where there is a clash between due process and crime control. Due process wants greater disclosure. Crime control wants less and emphasises how cases have had to be dropped because of refusal to reveal the names of informers and how this is being exploited by the defence.

(g) Quality of lawyers and judges. More effective training has been recommended by the Royal Commission on Criminal Justice. However, most defendants are represented by lawyers who are paid by legal aid. Unless legal aid rates are substantially increased then it is unlikely that the quality of the legal representation would dramatically improve.

Conclusion

Analysing a criminal justice system by reference to due process and crime control values is a useful way of assessing the system. However, because the objectives are potentially conflicting, all that can be achieved is an uneasy balancing of these two value systems. The reality actually becomes a continuing conflict between the two, like a never-ending game of tennis where one value system will be winning or given emphasis for a while only to find that the other value is fighting back.

QUESTION 2

Distinguish between the inquisitorial style of criminal procedure and the adversarial system. Consider the advantages and disadvantages of both systems and assess which style would serve justice better.

Commentary

In all systems there is the possibility of miscarriages of justice. It was the adversarial system that failed to do justice in a number of serious cases which came to light in the early 1990s. These scandals showed that there had been perjurious policemen, unfair prosecutors, deceitful scientists and biased judges. The adversarial nature of proceedings was not able to compensate for them, and the trial process and the appeal process were not able to recognise that these were miscarriages of justice. It is very doubtful that an inquisitorial system would have achieved better results. This is because such systems tend to give even more weight to the conclusions of policemen, scientists, lawyers and judges.

Suggested Answer

Adversarial Proceedings

In this system the parties play a dominant role. The adversarial nature of proceedings means that the onus of preparation is on the parties, and the trial judge is passive and functions like an umpire. The trial judge listens to the evidence and arguments produced by the two parties.

In criminal proceedings the investigatory work will be undertaken by the police. It is felt that the police have a tendency to become psychologically committed to the guilt of their chosen suspect. This is also true of prosecutors. The parties decide what witnesses to call and in what order. The parties examine and cross-examine the witnesses and if both sides decide not to call a witness, even if that witness may have relevant evidence, then the court generally cannot do anything about it. There is a danger in the common law systems that the evidence of a particular witness may become suppressed either because one side contrives to suppress or because neither side wishes to call that witness.

The function of the adversary system is to test a criminal charge according to the very high standard of proof beyond reasonable doubt. This is designed to protect the innocent by protecting those who are probably (but not certainly) guilty as well. This standard of proof is necessary but it is not a sufficient safeguard against wrong convictions. In addition there need to be effective procedural safeguards against certain types of evidence and certain kinds of prosecution behaviour because they have caused wrong convictions. The adversarial nature of proceedings will only work effectively if there is equality between the prosecution and defence. However, the prosecution often have an advantage because they have more resources than defendants and legal aid has proved to be inadequate especially in the areas of forensic science. In the Birmingham six case the defence forensic scientist could not carry out tests to back up his theory that the test used to show that defendants had handled explosives was misleading. Because of this deficiency the trial judge said that he preferred the evidence of the prosecution forensic scientist.

Since the Police and Criminal Evidence Act 1984, s. 58, most suspects at police stations have had a qualified right of access to a solicitor. This is reinforced by a duty solicitor scheme. These safeguards are designed to protect suspects in the police station.

Inquisitorial Proceedings

In inquisitorial proceedings a dominant role is played by the court. The judge calls the witnesses and examines them, while the parties or their lawyers play a supporting or subsidiary role, suggesting the names of further witnesses to call and asking questions after the court has finished asking its questions.

A dossier is prepared which is read by the presiding judge before the trial and is used as the basis for calling and questioning witnesses. There is a concern that the case would be prejudged because of the contents of the dossier.

About 10 per cent of cases in France are prepared by a quasi-judicial figure called the *juge d'instruction* (examining magistrate). The rest are prepared by the police. Because a suspect must be questioned so as to build up the dossier it is common for suspects to spend lengthy periods in pre-charge detention to assist in this process, for the first 48 hours generally without access to a lawyer. There is a great danger that confessions obtained after long periods of isolated custody are unreliable. There are no time limits on remands in custody and there seem to be long delays in the system.

Which is Better?

The traditional English approach is that truth is best discovered by powerful arguments from both parties which are then evaluated by a passive and impartial adjudicator. This approach acknowledges that the events leading up to a criminal offence, and the intentions or knowledge of the parties involved, are always open to interpretation and dispute.

The danger with the inquisitorial system is that the person conducting the investigation may come to a particular view and draw conclusions from that view without considering other possibilities — a bit like it is suggested that the police do in the UK. But in the inquisitorial system there are not the British safeguards that have been built up in recognition of that problem. Also it would seem that it is difficult for the defence to work out in some situations whether the dossier contains all that it should. The trial judge may come to a particular view based on reading the dossier which then forms his or her approach at trial.

In both systems sight of the truth can be lost. In the inquisitorial system the way in which the search for evidence is conducted can shape what is found. In the adversarial system one or both of the parties might deliberately suppress relevant evidence for tactical reasons or the defence might lack adequate access to the resources or expertise needed to counterbalance the arguments of their opponent. Therefore neither system is superior in establishing the truth.

The adversarial system accepts the reality that the State is trying to prove a case against a person. It accepts that guarantees are needed to stop the State abusing its investigative powers and that the means are provided to suspects to challenge the prosecution case. In recognition of this, defence lawyers play a central role and there are strict time limits in which a person can be held by the police for questioning. The lack of procedural safeguards in the inquisitorial system is justified on the basis that they hamper the search for the truth.

Conclusion

Both systems are concerned with finding the truth but each go about it in a different way. Both have advantages and disadvantages. The English criminal justice system has been adversarial in nature for hundreds of years and that system has become so deeply ingrained that it is too late to change it. Further the inquisitorial system is not so overwhelmingly better as to be attractive. On the contrary there is a fear that it does a better job of hiding its miscarriages of justice.

Both Royal Commissions considered the merits of the inquisitorial system but both came to the view that changing to it would be too fundamental to be practical. There were also doubts about whether the fusion of the functions of investigation and prosecution and the direct involvement of judges would be more likely to serve the interests of justice than a system in which the role of the police, prosecutors and judges are as far as possible kept separate. A system of separate roles offers better protection for the innocent defendant.

The Royal Commission on Criminal Justice was of the view that all adversarial systems contain inquisitorial elements and vice versa. It was of the view that some of its recommendations were a move to an inquisitorial system or at least an attempt to minimise the danger of adversarial practices being taken too far.

QUESTION 3

The creation of the Criminal Cases Review Commission and changing the powers of the Court of Appeal are important steps in improving the process by which miscarriages of justice are rectified. To what extent do you agree with this point of view?

Commentary

This question accepts that there will always be miscarriages of justice and therefore post-trial machinery for their rectification is necessary. If such machinery is to work effectively then it needs the resources to investigate and rectify miscarriages of justice. The question asks for an assesment of whether the new system will be adequate.

Suggested Answer

The Royal Commission on Criminal Justice recommended strengthening the powers of the Court of Appeal to quash convictions that are considered to be unsafe and for the establishment of a Criminal Cases Review Commission which would refer cases back to the Court of Appeal for reconsideration.

Strengthening the Powers of the Court of Appeal (Criminal Division)

There has been academic speculation about whether the Court of Appeal's powers have really been strengthened. It has been felt that the Court of Appeal has in certain situations taken a restrictive approach towards the exercise of its powers. The old law contained in the Criminal Appeal Act 1968, s. 2(1), was that an appeal against conviction would be allowed if all the circumstances of the case showed that the conviction was unsafe and unsatisfactory, or that the trial judge made a wrong decision on any question of law or there was a material irregularity in the course of the trial. These were the only allowable grounds of appeal and there was a proviso to s. 2(1) which said that even though the appeal raised points in the appellant's favour the appeal could still be dismissed if the Court of Appeal was of the view that no miscarriage of justice had actually happened. Critics of this section were of the view that it was difficult to reconcile the grounds of appeal with the proviso. This is why the majority of the Royal Commission recommended a single ground of appeal. The Criminal Appeal Act 1995 introduces an unsafeness test. The Court of Appeal must allow an appeal against conviction if it thinks that the conviction is unsafe and must dismiss an appeal in any other case.

This would mean that if there is a doubt whether the appellant committed the offence which is the subject of the conviction then the Court of Appeal would quash the conviction. If the Court of Appeal adopted the approach that it will not quash a conviction if something may have gone wrong at or before the trial but there is no doubt that the appellant is guilty then this could be an even more restrictive approach. This is why Professor Zander dissented because he felt the integrity of the system had to be considered when deciding whether to quash a conviction. Views have differed on whether the word 'unsatisfactory' does add anything. In *R* v *McIlkenny* (1991) 93 Cr app R 287 (the Birmingham six), counsel for the Director of Public Prosecutions conceded that the convictions were unsatisfactory but argued that they were not necessarily unsafe. However, the Court of Appeal said that whether there was a difference between the two words had never been decided by any court and there was no reason to decide the question in this case. It may become clearer in the years ahead whether the word 'unsatisfactory' is mere surplusage or whether its repeal will restrict the powers of the court to quash convictions. The Royal Commission on Criminal Justice felt that the correct approach is that if a conviction is or may be unsafe then it should be quashed. The government refused to give in to strong pressure from the Bar, Law Society and civil liberty groups such as Liberty who all argued that the Court of Appeal should be required to quash a conviction which is or may be unsafe. The Lord Chief Justice speaking in the House of Lords on the Bill's second reading was of the view that 'is unsafe' is a satisfactory statutory test and that it would include 'or may be unsafe' because a conviction which may be unsafe is unsafe.

Thus there is a dispute about whether the test in the Criminal Appeal Act 1995 is narrower than that recommended by the Royal Commission on Criminal Justice.

Criminal Cases Review Commission

This body is independent of both the courts and the Home Office. The powers that this body has are contained in the Criminal Appeal Act 1995. It can investigate controversial convictions and refer them back to the Court of Appeal as soon as real doubt has been established. However, the organisation Justice fears that flaws in the Act may compromise its independence and effectiveness. These flaws concern the conduct of investigations and the appointment of members. The members of the Commission would be government appointees and instead of having its own core of investigators the Commission will refer inquiries to the police. Justice is of the view that there are three crucial elements that will decide whether it will be effective. These are:

(a)   The integrity of the investigative process.

(b)   The robustness of the Commission's members.

(c)   The power of disclosure to and from the Criminal Cases Review Commission.

The fact that the police will be doing the investigation has been severely criticised. Chris Mullin MP, who campaigned on behalf of the Birmingham six, has stated that this is a fatal flaw. It would be far better for there to be some independent investigators employed direct by the Commission. This is because a wrongful conviction will usually result from errors either in the police investigation or the legal process. The investigating officer is under no duty to pass on the evidence accumulated during the inquiries, but only needs to prepare a report. The Act makes no financial provision for police inquiries. Police budgets are now capped and there may be difficulties allocating substantial resources to carrying out such investigations.

The government's response to the above criticisms has been that Commission members will be appointed after public advertisements and according to job description.

Reasons why the New Body is Better than the Old Arrangements

It may be that people who have suffered a miscarriage of justice will not even get leave to appeal. This certainly happened in some of the miscarriage of justice cases such as the Tottenham three and the Guildford four. Even with leave to appeal, the Court of Appeal may not realise that a miscarriage of justice has happened. A convicted person who is granted leave to appeal is only entitled to one appeal (*R* v *Pinfold* [1988] QB 462). In the past, the only other way to get before the Court of Appeal was by a Home Secretary's reference.

The Criminal Appeal Act 1995 abolishes the Home Secretary's reference and replaces it with the Criminal Cases Review Commission.

The Home Secretary's reference has been criticised for the following reasons. It only applied with regard to Crown Court trials. The Home Secretary would normally only refer if there was new evidence or some other consideration of substance that was not before the trial court. Successive Home Secretaries had taken a very cautious approach because of both the political considerations and constitutional principles. The political consideration is not to be seen to be soft on crime. The constitutional considerations concern the separation of powers and it must not be thought that a Minister is telling the courts what to do. It was thought constitutionally wrong for Ministers to suggest to the Court of Appeal that courts should have reached different decisions. Home Secretaries have also taken the view that there is no purpose in referring a case where there is no real possibility of the Court of Appeal taking a different view than it did on the original appeal because of the lack of fresh evidence or some other new consideration of substance.

Conclusion

The creation of a Criminal Cases Review Commission is essential if the legal system is to provide a remedy for innocent victims of the system. However, the body will not help to reduce the number of innocent victims. Only reforms elsewhere in the criminal justice system would do that. The creation of this body is only a modest advance to provide a remedy for miscarriages after they have taken place, preferably before the victim has completed the prison sentence or a substantial amount of it. It has to be realised that it is more important to put in place reforms that would reduce the risk of a miscarriage of justice in the first place.

9 The Criminal Justice System: Mixed Aspects

INTRODUCTION

This chapter contains mixed questions about judges, magistrates, juries and miscarriages of justice.

QUESTION 1

Trial by jury is central to the criminal justice system and as a guardian of due process and civil liberties. Discuss.

Commentary

This question concerns the jury and how it fits in with the objectives and general principles of the criminal justice system.

Suggested Answer

Due process principles emphasise procedural safeguards and procedural fairness. A guardian of due process and civil liberties would be a protector of the right to a fair trial, a protection against oppressive prosecutions, and also a counterbalance against unfair procedures or procedures weighted in favour of the prosecution at the pre-trial stage.

Are Jury Trials Central to the Criminal Justice System?

Whether the jury is central is a moot point. It depends on the meaning of 'central'. Over 95 per cent of criminal cases are dealt with in the magistrates' courts. Therefore if volume is the criterion for determining centrality then the jury is not central. Trial by magistrates is increasingly common because, in recent years, more offences have been reclassified as summary only.

However, trial by jury is the method of trial for the most serious offences and in that sense is central to the criminal justice system. Liberty would agree with this definition. Further they would argue that too many offences have been made summary only and should at least be restored to triable either way with defendants having a right to elect for trial by jury.

Is the Jury a Counterweight for Pre-trial Unfairness?

Although juries were not directly blamed for the miscarriage of justice cases of the 1970s, it may be said that unreliable evidence before a court is likely to lead to an unreliable result. Another reason why the jury should not be blamed is because a number of the trial judges involved clearly indicated either in their summing up or when sentencing that they favoured the prosecution evidence. Whatever the method of adjudication it can be argued that the results would have been the same. However, one effect of the miscarriage of justice cases is that there is evidence that juries since then have been more reluctant to convict on confession evidence alone. The miscarriage of justice cases show that juries were not able to protect against pre-trial misconduct although there is evidence that they are more alert to the possibility today.

Does the Jury Safeguard Civil Liberties?

Section 8 of the Contempt of Court Act 1981 forbids direct research into the jury. Therefore one can only consider some of the highly publicised cases. There is certainly evidence of jury equity or jury nullification which means that juries acquit in the face of evidence that indicates guilt. The cases demonstrating this include the case of Randle and Pottle, the Cyprus spy trial, the Clive Ponting case, and the eighteenth-century sheep-stealing cases. Jury equity has been accepted as a role of the jury over the centuries.

When considering whether the jury is a safeguard of due process and civil liberties it must be realised that this should cover all citizens. But it may be questioned whether British citizens of Afro-Caribbean origin benefit, for example, when a black defendant faces an all-white jury. *R v Ford* [1989] QB 868 is an example of that. Ford was black and was tried for a motoring offence yet was not comfortable facing an all-white jury. The Court of Appeal was not prepared to introduce the principle of a multiracial jury.

There is a concern about the role of juries in complex and long cases. The concern is whether juries can really understand the issues and come to reliable verdicts. If they cannot do this then the jury is not a protector of due process and a guardian of civil liberties for all defendants in serious complex cases.

Problems that Jury Convictions Cause for Appeals

Rights of appeal are limited because there is the principle that the verdict of a jury is sacrosanct. The conviction can only be challenged if one can point to a material irregularity in the trial, the admission of inadmissible evidence, or an error in the judge's directions on points of law that make the conviction unsafe. If the trial has been conducted properly and there is a conviction there is nothing that can be done. Generally the Court of Appeal does not feel that it can intervene when the jury's verdict of guilty is surprising in the light of the evidence. Juries do not give reasons for their verdicts so it is impossible to know whether they took wrong considerations into account. There is concern that the jury system will be undermined if the Court of Appeal were to second-guess jury verdicts when the defence cannot point to anything specifically wrong with the trial and there was evidence on which the jury was entitled to convict. The jury is an unwieldy and cumbersome institution and prevents a more flexible approach to trial such as more adjournments or giving reasons for a verdict.

Conclusion

It is the argument of the civil liberty groups that trial by jury is a guardian of due process and civil liberties. However, there has been a realisation as a result of the miscarriage of justice cases that it is difficult for a jury to protect against an absence of due process safeguards elsewhere in the criminal justice system. Despite this, the jury is most definitely a due process input and it does provide a balance in the criminal justice system. Although juries have not been able to prevent all miscarriages of justice it can be argued that miscarriages of justice might increase if the jury is no longer there.

QUESTION 2

Assess the advantages and disadvantages of the proposal that all trials should be conducted by a single professional judge sitting alone.

Commentary

This question concerns an evaluation of the respective merits of the jury, lay magistracy and the professional judiciary.

Sometimes in exams reference will be made to lay participation in the criminal justice system, which would include a discussion of both the jury and the lay magistrates.

Suggested Answer

There are two courts of trial for criminal matters: magistrates' courts and the Crown Court. In both there is lay participation. In the magistrates' courts, lay magistrates sit in benches of three, although trials in London and other major cities may be conducted by a single professional judge known as a stipendiary magistrate. All trials in the Crown Court are conducted by a judge and jury.

There is trial by judge and jury in a few civil matters mainly in the High Court concerning defamation, malicious prosecution, false imprisonment and fraud.

Advantages of Trial by a Professional Judge Alone

A judge is generally better than lay persons in weighing up issues and applying the law to the facts. There would be better quality justice with higher standards of experience, expertise and legal abilities, and trials can be carried out more quickly and more efficiently. It is often thought that trial by lay magistrates is the cheapest form of trial because they are volunteers. However, probably today a single professional judge would be cheaper or as cheap as lay magistrates because magistrates still have to be paid travelling allowances, loss of earnings allowances and they are much slower. Taking this all together it is believed that a single professional judge would be cheaper and more efficient.

The former chief of the Metropolitan police, Sir Robert Mark, in the Richard Dimbleby lecture in 1973, criticised juries for their refusal to convict and for acquittals which were blatantly perverse. He was clearly of the view that the acquittal rates were too high and the fault for this was with the jury. The Clive Ponting case has been used by critics as an example of juries not acting in accordance with the evidence. This problem would be resolved with a single professional judge. Further if trial is by a single professional judge it would be possible to give the prosecution a right to appeal against acquittals. Currently there is no such prosecution right of appeal because of the principle of the sanctity of the jury verdict.

Both lay magistrates and the jury do not give reasons for their decisions. A single professional judge would be able to do so.

Disadvantages of Trial by a Professional Judge Alone

The greatest disadvantage is that this would be the end of the lay principle. Even if instead it was decided that a professional judge should sit with two lay assessors this would still be a different working of the lay principle as presently understood. There is greater accountability with a jury because every prosecution in the Crown Court has to be justified to 12 jurors or at least 10 out of 12 generally.

A judge cannot do 'jury equity', that is, acquitting when the evidence shows factual and legal guilt. However, some may believe that this is an advantage because it is not for the jury to take the law into its own hands but for Parliament to change the law. In reality it means that the law in an individual case can never go beyond the tolerance level of the jury. Further the jury collectively has a wider experience of the world than the judge. Many members of the jury will only earn a fraction of the judge's salary and live quite different lifestyles and be able to understand the lifestyles and standards of conduct of those on trial.

Further there is a division of labour between the jury and the trial judge that would be lost if a single professional judge is introduced, namely, that the judge decides questions of admissibility of evidence in the absence of the jury and the jury then decides guilt or innocence on the basis of the admissible evidence alone. The advantage of this division is that the jury never knows about the inadmissible evidence and so is not affected by it. In the magistrates' court the magistrates hear the applications for exclusion of evidence but if it is excluded they have heard it and one has to guess to what extent this has an effect in real terms on the magistrates. If there is a single professional judge then it has to be considered whether all questions of admissibility should be dealt with at a pre-trial stage before another judge who does not become the trial judge should evidence be held to be inadmissible.

Civil trials

A single professional judge could easily take over the functions of the jury in civil cases. This would be an advantage because civil juries are often criticised for too high awards of damages. The only disadvantage of a single professional judge in defamation cases is that it is the jury's function to assess whether the words amounted to defamation which ordinary people might best know.

Conclusion

Really the choice is between efficiency and cheapness which are the advantages of the single professional judge and on the other hand the principle of the lay input. Whilst change to a single professional judge does seem radical it is something that could be easily implemented. It is the radicalness that will hold back this idea. However, the Roskill Committee on Fraud Trials suggested that for serious fraud there should be a single professional judge with two lay assessors and thought that this idea could apply to other types of offences. There is a feeling that this will be a halfway measure for a start but would eventually give way to single professional judges.

QUESTION 3

It is impossible to defend the system by which judges and magistrates are appointed. An independent judicial commission is needed which should be given responsibility for all matters relating to the appointment, training, discipline and removal of judges and magistrates and promotion of judges. Discuss.

Commentary

This question requires a consideration of the way judges and magistrates are appointed, trained, disciplined and removed and whether a judicial commission might be a more effective way of dealing with these matters than the present arrangements.

Suggested Answer

The statement made in the question is an extreme statement to the effect that nothing good can be said in favour of the existing appointment system, so much so that the system needs radical reform and cannot be supported in the face of severe criticism. It is necessary to examine the appointments systems for both the lay magistracy and the professional judiciary.

The main criticism of appointment of the professional judiciary is that in effect it is a private system of appointments with too much power in the hands of one person, namely, the Lord Chancellor and, for the senior appointments, in the ultimate hands of the Prime Minister. The main criticisms are that for the High Court bench and above, appointment is by invitation only, and that generally the system works by word of mouth. A secret file is built up over many years including assessment of judicial work in a part-time capacity. The benefit of such an approach is that this a better way of assessing a person's true character than a simple interview. Also the part-time appointment system saves money because part-time judges are cheaper than full-time judges, for example, they are not entitled to any pension rights. But the drawback is that these judges have no security of tenure and the invitation can just lapse. Another criticism of the appointment system is that solicitors, women and minorities are insufficiently represented on the professional bench.

For appointments to the lay magistracy the Lord Chancellor relies on recommendations from local advisory committees from around the country. That method of selection also puts heavy reliance on word of mouth recommendations which has the tendency to lead to appointments of mainly middle-class persons.

An Independent Judicial Commission

The benefits of an independent judicial commission would be that a whole range of people could make up the commission including lay people. The composition could include judges, barristers, solicitors, women and members of the ethnic minorities. Applicants could apply and they would be interviewed by a commission panel. This would eliminate the criticisms that recommendation for appointment is by word of mouth, that appointments are by invitation only, and that there is too much power in one pair of hands.

However Lord Taylor of Gosforth, the Lord Chief Justice, believes that a judicial appointments commission will be no better than the present system because the lay members would have little direct knowledge of the candidates and interview by such a commission would not be as good a screening process as the present system. Lord Taylor is also of the view that the problem of not enough women and people from the ethnic minorities will change in due course as more women and ethnic minorities come to practise at the Bar.

Another problem with a judicial commission would be its membership. A public figure would be needed as chair and it is argued that if all judicial appointments are to be dealt with by the commission it would be difficult to find someone who would be prepared to take on such an appointment because it would be so time consuming. Further if lay people are involved one wonders how they could make as good a choice as the Lord Chancellor.

The Judges' Council is against a judicial appointments commission, because of concerns that places on the commission could be awarded for political reasons and that the judges might lose their centuries-old right to pass on an approved list of potential judges to the Lord Chancellor.

Promotion to a higher judicial rank is done in the same secretive way as appointment to the judiciary. Therefore if appointment as a judge in the first place would benefit from a judicial commission approach then so would promotions.

Training

The judicial commission could also take over the arrangements for training. There is a belief that training for the judiciary needs to be substantially increased. The Judicial Studies Board is currently responsible for training but it lacks resources. One concern is finding trainers. If judges are trainers then they would be taken away from judicial work and so would the judges attending the courses. The taking over of training by a judicial commission would establish the principle that there should be substantial training and also the need for comprehensive special training programmes for judges who are going to be doing specialist work, for example, the Serious Fraud Office in its submissions to the Royal Commission on Criminal Justice argued that judges needed more training concerning the handing of complex fraud trials. Pressure is building up for more training both for civil and criminal work. Further it is felt that should judges be expected to be trial managers for civil matters, managing cases, setting time limits and identifying key issues, then training would be crucial for carrying out these roles effectively.

There needs to be a new radical approach to judicial training. The most effective way to do this would be through a new body with a dynamic forward-looking composition which would really be prepared to work out detailed training programmes for the judges.

Monitoring, Discipline and Removal

This is a sensitive area because of the potential for interference with the independence of the judiciary. The current arrangements for removal of the judiciary at the High Court level and above are considered to protect the independence of the judiciary. There has to be an address of both houses of Parliament before there can be a removal. This has never been used in the twentieth century. It was only used once in the nineteenth century to remove a judge in Ireland who had been convicted of appropriating for his own use funds paid into court. The circuit judiciary and below do not have this security of tenure protection and can be dismissed by the Lord Chancellor. This was done in 1983, when Judge Bruce Campbell was convicted of smuggling whisky and cigarettes into Britain in his yacht. Judge Pickles, a circuit judge, wrote in his book *Straight from the Bench* (1987) that he was threatened with dismissal. He describes how judges are controlled. He says control is by an old-boy approach of 'don't let down the side' and also by being able to withhold favours such as promotion, honours, and membership of royal commissions which are all in the gift of the Lord Chancellor. Pickles is of the view that these promotions and favours create holds over persons who want such things.

Pickles was threatened with dismissal because he had written an article published in the *Daily Telegraph* entitled 'A place for punishment'. The Lord Chancellor, Lord Hailsham of St Marylebone, thought that writing a newspaper article, even one carefully written, can amount to misbehaviour sufficient to warrant dismissal. Pickles's reply in 1985 made the point that the Lord Chancellor was complainant, prosecutor, judge and jury. He felt that this could not be right and would not have public support. It went against elementary principles of natural justice including the right to a fair hearing.

Pickles was of the view that Parliament should define misbehaviour. However, the production of a definition would be the perfect work for a judicial commission. As a result of pressure the Lord Chancellor has been working on a definition. In 1994 the Lord Chancellor announced that misbehaviour would include convictions for driving while under the influence of alcohol or drugs, offences of violence to persons, dishonesty or moral depravity. Further, that racial, religious or sexual harassment is not consistent with the standards expected of those who hold judicial office.

In the United States of America and Canada, there are various structures for considering complaints, and decisions are made by committees which include both judicial and lay representation. Procedural fairness is guaranteed to those whose conduct is under investigation. It is becoming increasingly untenable that standards of judicial discipline and conduct should be left to a government Minister and the civil servants in his department. Effective judicial administration requires the development of a code of conduct to lay down the ethical standards that the judiciary should follow in a variety of different situations.

There is an argument that monitoring the performance of judges might affect their independence. Despite that fact, the Royal Commission on Criminal Justice recommended that there should be judicial monitoring and it is arguable that this will not affect independence because there is a sharp distinction between the independence of the judiciary, which must be upheld, and the efficiency of the courts and the judiciary system which is appropriate for monitoring. An independent judicial commission is ideal for arranging and analysing such monitoring in such a way as to safeguard the independence of the judiciary. The Royal Commission suggested that monitoring could be carried out by retired judges. This could be done under the auspices of the commission.

Lay Magistrates

If we are to continue with lay magistrates then a judicial commission might be able to devise a better method of recommending appointments. The present system of local advisory committees has not solved the problem of too many middle-class Conservative voters becoming lay magistrates. Perhaps there could be a judicial commission representative appointed to each local committee to oversee and ensure that they are using proper appointment methods. However, the commission would still need to rely on some form of local advisory committees because of the large number of appointments — about 2,000 to 3,000 per year.

A commission would be able to make better national planning arrangements for the training of the magistrates and argue for more resources to be devoted to training. It would be better able to keep under review training procedures and might be able to combine some advanced training on new legislation with other members of the judiciary.

With regard to discipline and removal the current position is similar to that of circuit judges and below, i.e., the Lord Chancellor makes the ultimate decision. For the same reasons as stated above this is unsatisfactory and a judicial commission would be able to devise fairer procedures.

Conclusion

Everything about the current arrangements is amateurish and haphazard. The main benefit of a judicial commission responsible for all matters is that it could aim to introduce as many modern methods of appointment as is possible and also to have modern methods of disciplining those who do not come up to the required standards.

QUESTION 4

There is nothing wrong with the criminal jury trial which cannot be put right by improving the law, the procedures, evidence, the role of the judge, the lawyers, the prosecuting authorities, in short, everything else in the criminal justice system. Discuss.

Commentary

This question requires a consideration of whether the deficiencies that can be identified concerning the jury can actually be overcome by improving other aspects of the criminal justice system.

Suggested Answer

Deficiencies of Trial by Jury

The main concern is whether the jury really can understand the issues that are being dealt with in long and complicated cases, especially fraud. If they cannot understand the evidence then it must be doubted whether they can come to a decision that is consistent with it. Worse than that, a trial might collapse and have to be stopped halfway because of the jury. For example, in 1995 in the case of *R* v *O'Callaghan* the trial judge ruled that the evidence was too difficult for the jury to understand and stopped the case.

The time taken for long trials means that they are heard by unrepresentative juries consisting only of people available to sit for such a long trial. Cost and length are other factors undermining the arguments for a jury in these cases.

Improving the Law

It has been argued that the actual offence of fraud is too complicated and that the law should be simplified in this area. Other areas of the law that have been criticised are the law on manslaughter and the Offences against the Person Act 1861. There is a view that the criminal law should be codified. The Law Commission has drafted a criminal code but Parliament has never made the time to consider it.

Improving the Procedures and the Evidence

Greater assistance to the jury would be helpful such as the use of computers to display documents on screen which would both speed up the trial and help understanding. In the 1995 trial of the Maxwell brothers the 25,000-page trial bundle was scanned and recorded on to two CDs shortly before trial. This enabled documents referred to in court to appear on the courtroom's 18 monitors. The documents could be enlarged or highlighted as required. This has made referring to documents and the evidence much easier and more effective.

In 1995 the Association of Chief Police Officers (ACPO) released the results of some research that it had been carrying out. The research made a detailed examination of criminal proceedings for serious offences in England and Wales and concluded that too many cases fail because crucial evidence is ruled inadmissible, that judges are overcautious when deciding questions of admissibility and that defence lawyers exploit technicalities. The police want changes in the rules of evidence to permit more evidence to be admissible before the jury, for example, that it would be more easily possible to adduce evidence before the jury of an accused's previous convictions.

Role of the Judge

The judge has to explain the law and the issues to the jury, rule on the admissibility of evidence, for example, confession evidence, and ensure that the proceedings are conducted fairly according to the rules of evidence and the law. At the close of the prosecution and defence case it is the judge's function to sum up to the jury. This is a very important role and it is crucial that a judge should be properly trained and competent to perform this function. There has been criticism in recent years that judges are not adequately trained for this function. Judges now receive specific training in how to sum up to the jury. Serious fraud cases require greater skills on the judge's part and there is a view that only the more skilled and most senior of judges should preside in these cases. There have been calls for judges to be given specific training on accounting procedures and standards, and reading and understanding complicated financial documents. There also needs to be a greater knowledge and understanding of forensic evidence. There is also a feeling that if judges took greater control of the trial proceedings by imposing conditions on the prosecution such as limiting the number of counts that they can proceed with at trial then that would cut down the length of trials to more manageable lengths.

The Lawyers

Both prosecution and defence lawyers work in an adversarial system, which means the onus of preparing for the trial is primarily on them. There has been a growing realisation that the quality of lawyers and the quality of their preparation has an influence on the outcome of the case. The other role of the lawyers is to present the case clearly to the court. As they are officers of the court they should not mislead the jury. There is a view that sometimes defence lawyers try to confuse the jury, which is something that the trial judge should try to stop.

There can be some defence inadequacies. Defences may not be properly prepared. This can be due to various factors but one would be the lack of legal aid which most defendants rely on. If legal aid is not adequate then preparation and presentation of the defence case may be weaker. This causes problems in carrying out the necessary investigation work which may be further hampered by the client being in prison prior to the trial.

Most trial work is carried out by barristers who are instructed by solicitors. The defence barrister's performance may be affected by various factors which include lack of experience or competence, and late delivery of the brief. In many cases the legally aided defendant meets his or her barrister for the first time on the morning of the trial. Tactical mistakes may be made or there may be a failure to appreciate a potentially crucial aspect of the case. The Court of

Appeal has been reluctant to quash convictions on the ground of misguided or less than desired legal work, requiring flagrantly incompetent advocacy to justify interference with the verdict. The Royal Commission on Criminal Justice believed this was too strict a standard and that the Court of Appeal should be more prepared to consider whether errors of legal judgment and inadequacy in a lawyer's performance may have led to a wrongful conviction.

However, the Royal Commission's solution was to recommend that barristers should be personally penalised. It suggested that a trial judge who thought that counsel was wasting the court's time should recommend a reduction of the barrister's fee or order that he or she should pay the prosecution's costs. This could have the effect in some cases of a defence lawyer being deterred from pressing a case in the face of a hostile judge.

Prosecuting Authorities

Prosecuting authorities include the police, the Crown Prosecution Service and the barristers or solicitor advocates who may be instructed by the Crown Prosecution Service to undertake advocacy in the Crown Court. Police work is crucial because if they provide unreliable or distorted evidence then that leads to unreliable evidence being put before the jury which could lead to an unreliable result. The Royal Commission on Criminal Justice has recommended that the police receive better training in effective interviewing techniques. The Crown Prosecution Service was created so that there could be greater professionalism in prosecuting cases. That would include reviewing all prosecutions to decide whether there is sufficient evidence and whether the prosecution is in the public interest.

Conclusion

If there could be a substantial raising of standards in all the other organisations in the criminal justice system then there would be a greater chance that the jury would understand the issues and come to an appropriate and correct verdict. Therefore looked at in that light certainly if other areas of the criminal justice system were improved then things that are considered to be wrong with the criminal jury system would be reduced or eliminated. However, it would still have to be proved that juries could really understand the issues, follow the evidence, and were representative.

Thus improving the competency of the other participants in the criminal justice system may help in the majority of cases. But in serious fraud cases one of the problems is the excessive length of the trial process itself. That might be an area which cannot always be put right merely by improving the quality of the other participants in the criminal justice system. Further there is a limit to simplification.

It may be that removing juries from serious fraud cases would not substantially reduce their length because witnesses still have to be cross-examined. A single professional judge or a judge and two expert lay assessors may have higher conviction rates than juries and this may persuade more defendants to plead guilty and take the discount on sentence which is usually given for a guilty plea.

10 Police Powers

INTRODUCTION

This chapter consists of essay-type questions on the arrest and detention provisions of the Police and Criminal Evidence Act 1984 (PACE 1984). There is also a question on the important discretion conferred on trial judges enabling the exclusion of otherwise admissible evidence under s. 78 of PACE 1984.

You should be aware of the main themes of crime control and the due process model when considering the criminal justice system and how PACE 1984 functions in that context.

There have been some changes concerning police powers made by the Criminal Justice and Public Order Act 1994. The significant change is in s. 60 which gives the police powers to stop and search in anticipation of violence. Where violence may take place a senior police officer, generally of the rank of superintendent or above, can authorise the stopping and searching of persons and vehicles within a particular locality for a period not exceeding 24 hours which can be extended for a further six hours. Where s. 60 has been invoked, a constable in uniform can stop and search any pedestrian or vehicle for offensive weapons or dangerous instruments. Any person or vehicle can be stopped even if the police have no suspicion that the person or vehicle is carrying any offensive weapons or dangerous instruments. If any such things are found then the police can seize them. Any person who fails to stop when required by a constable is guilty of an offence.

QUESTION 1

Distinguish between the circumstances which justify an arrest by a police officer for arrestable and non-arrestable offences.

Commentary

The start of the criminal process will generally be an arrest when there has been a reasonable suspicion that an offence has been or is about to be committed or is actually in the process of being committed. Proper procedures are required to prevent a police policy of 'round up anyone you see' or 'round up the usual suspects'.

Suggested Answer

There are two basic ways in which an arrest may be made. First in execution of a warrant and second without a warrant but pursuant to statute or common law.

Arrest by Warrant

A warrant is issued by a magistrate (Magistrates' Court Act 1980, s. 1) on being satisfied with the case proposed by the police. A warrant is appropriate where the police want to arrest a named person with regard to an arrestable offence. The actual offence must be specified in the warrant. Warrants are nowadays mainly used when a suspect fails to appear in court to answer a summons or to answer bail.

Arrest without Warrant

Arrest powers would not be adequate if people could only be arrested by warrant. Arrest without warrant is necessary because there is a need to stop immediately people who are about to commit crimes or who are in the act of committing them. There is also a need to be able to arrest without warrant those who have committed crimes because they might use the time lapse that would be involved in obtaining a warrant for making an escape. Arrest by warrant is cumbersome for modern policing practices and inhibits quick responses for ensuring the protection of the public.

Statutory Arrest Powers without Warrant

PACE 1984 lays down powers to arrest persons in relation to arrestable and non-arrestable offences. An arrestable offence is one where the sentence is fixed by law or where the person can be sentenced to a five-year term of imprisonment, for example, murder and theft. Section 24(1) of the 1984 Act defines what offences are arrestable offences.

Section 24 of the 1984 Act provides for different categories of arrest power. Both police officers and citizens have the power of arrest but the powers to arrest are wider for police officers than for citizens.

Anyone may arrest a person who is committing an arrestable offence and anyone may arrest any person who is suspected on reasonable grounds of committing an arrestable offence (s. 24(4)).

Where an arrestable offence has been committed, any person may arrest anyone who is guilty of the offence, or any person who is suspected on reasonable grounds of having committed the offence (s. 24(5)).

Only a police officer can arrest a person on reasonable grounds for suspecting that an arrestable offence has been committed and he has reasonable grounds for suspecting that person to be guilty of the offence (s. 24(6)).

Only a police officer can arrest a person who is about to commit an arrestable offence, or any person who is suspected on reasonable grounds of being about to commit an arrestable offence (s. 24(7)).

The law is stricter about when persons who are not police officers can lawfully arrest. It was held in *R* v *Self* [1992] 1 WLR 692 that where a person who is not a constable reasonably suspects that an individual has committed an arrestable offence the arrest will be unlawful if no such offence has been committed.

In certain circumstances a police officer may arrest even though the offence is non-arrestable, for example, riding a bike without lights. A police officer can only do this if one or more of the arrest conditions in s. 25 apply. The arrest conditions that must be present before there can be a valid arrest include the fact that the name of the person is not known or readily ascertainable or there are reasonable grounds for doubting that the name the person has given is his or her real name, for example, he said his name is Ringo Starr, or that the address given is unsatisfactory or is doubted.

Other arrest conditions contained in s. 25 are that the arrest is necessary to prevent the arresting person from harming himself or others, suffering physical injury, causing loss of or damage to property, committing an offence against public decency or causing an unlawful obstruction of the highway, or it is necessary to protect a child or other vulnerable person from the person being arrested. The general arrest conditions in s. 25 are needed to ensure that suspects can be properly identified and also to deal with any immediate law and order concerns.

Common Law Powers to Arrest without Warrant

One of the main functions of the police is to maintain law and order. So there is a common law power of arrest for breach of the peace. Police can arrest if a breach of the peace is happening, or is about to happen or has recently happened and is likely to happen again (*R* v *Howell* [1982] QB 416).

In practice this power of arrest can be widely used because, although the Court of Appeal confirmed in *R* v *Howell* that a breach of a peace must be related to violence, it also happens when harm is done or is likely to be done or if someone fears that violence may happen. Therefore threatening, abusive or insulting behaviour may not of itself amount to a breach of the peace but it would if the police reasonably regard it as likely to cause imminent violence. Therefore the right to arrest for breach of the peace can be invoked during demonstrations, picketing, disputes between neighbours, and street brawls. It was also used in the miners' strike in the mid 1980s to turn back miners who were travelling to a coal mine to join a picket. They were told that if they did not turn back they would be arrested for a breach of the peace. It gives the police the power to say that if you do not do as I say I will arrest you for a breach of the peace. As the miners' strike in the mid 1980s showed this can be a powerful weapon in the police armoury.

Conclusion

The above discussion concerns the main powers of arrest. Today the warrant method is the least used of the methods of arrest. Arrest without warrant is a necessary power. So the only function of the law is to set limits so that the exercise of the powers to arrest are kept within the limits society can tolerate and accept.

QUESTION 2

'The innocent have nothing to fear from broad arrest powers' (Andrew Sanders and Richard Young, *Criminal Justice* (Butterworths)). Discuss.

Commentary

The above passage reflects the crime control model. What has to be considered is whether such a position in relation to arrest powers represents the present law, and whether the position expressed in the question should represent the law if it does not already.

Suggested Answer

The powers of arrest that are exercised today without warrant are mainly governed by the Police and Criminal Evidence Act 1984. The approach of PACE 1984 is very different from the early part of the nineteenth century when it was for magistrates to determine whether or not to prosecute. The decision was made by magistrates on information provided to them by the police and if magistrates were satisfied with the evidence they would issue a warrant for arrest. In the nineteenth century arrest was seen as a means of bringing offenders to court. Today arrest and subsequent detention are frequently used as part of the investigation and not as the culmination of it. PACE 1984 permits arrest without a prior warrant if an offence is an 'arrestable offence' pursuant to s. 24 of the Act. Arrestable offences include all offences punishable by a jail term of five years or more. The provisions in s. 24 ensure that the police may make arrests for arrestable offences whether actual or reasonably suspected and whether in the past, in the present or in the future.

Section 24(6) permits a constable to arrest even if no offence has been committed so long as the constable 'reasonably' suspects that the person being arrested has committed an offence. The powers of arrest are a clear manifestation of the crime control model with the means justifying the ends. The constable can arrest even on arbitrary grounds and the arrest can be justified so long as it turns out that the suspect was engaged in a crime.

PACE 1984 also permits arrest without warrant in respect of non-arrestable offences if certain circumstances referred to in the Act as general arrest conditions are present. Section 25 proceeds on the basis of certain subjective elements, that is, whether the constable believes that a summons cannot be served as it is impracticable or inappropriate. There is also an objective condition that the constable has 'reasonable grounds' for considering that an arrest condition applies. These include grounds for suspecting that a name furnished by the relevant person is not that person's real name and grounds for believing that the arrest is necessary to prevent circumstances identified in s. 25(3)(d).

It is interesting here to contrast s. 25 with s. 24 as in s. 24 the police can arrest for arrestable offences even when it is not necessary for them to do so. Arrests under s. 24 are made on reasonable suspicion and since that will not suffice to prosecute, the law envisages that the police have to get more evidence in order to prosecute.

In considering the crime control model in the area of arrests, it would be necessary to consider the remedy available to the citizen, which is a claim in damages for wrongful arrest. Wrongful arrest occurs when the powers discussed above are exceeded or when an arrest is unreasonable. When one is considering the principles of reasonableness it must be noted that a court would not intervene so long as the constable acts in a way that a reasonable man would act.

Taking a case that was before the 1984 Act one would see how broadly the police powers are interpreted. In *Holgate-Mohammed* v *Duke* [1984] AC 437, the suspect had allegedly sold stolen jewellery. The police had a description that fitted her and arrested on that reasonable suspicion. There was an action against the police for wrongful arrest on the basis that she could have been questioned equally well at home or at work. The police had conceded that arrest was not necessary, but in their view it was desirable as it was more likely that she would have confessed if she was questioned at the police station. The House of Lords declared that the question was whether the power to arrest was in accordance with the principle of reasonableness, and it was a question of considering whether any irrelevant facts were considered by the police in effecting the arrest. Consideration of where the suspect was most likely to confess was treated as a relevant factor. The case of *Holgate-Mohammed* v *Duke* shows that in a crime prevention model an arrest would not be treated as unlawful so long as it enhanced police efficiency.

The law imposes obligations on the police as well as an ordinary citizen to inform a person arrested of the grounds of arrest. Section 28 on first reading would suggest that there is a move towards due process since an arrest would be unlawful on the part of the police if a person is not informed of the reason for being arrested at the time of the arrest or as soon as reasonably practical after arrest.

However, from the House of Lords decision of *Murray* v *Ministry of Defence* [1988] 1 WLR 692, it would appear that the approach of the courts is to prefer a flexible approach that prefers crime control to due process. In *Murray*, a case from Northern Ireland, soldiers went to the home of the defendant and detained everyone and searched the premises at about 7.00 a.m. Only at 7.30 a.m. did the soldier in charge inform the defendant of her arrest and take her to an army detention centre.

This decision involved the issue of s. 14(2) of the Northern Ireland (Emergency Provisions) Act 1978 which requires a member of Her Majesty's Forces arresting a person while on duty to state that they were under arrest.

On the issue of breach of s. 14(2) it would appear that the arrest was unlawful from 7.00 a.m. to 7.30 a.m. since the defendant was not informed of her arrest. However, the House of Lords held that it was not practical to inform the defendant of her arrest as soon as the house was entered as there was a real risk of an alarm being raised. In those circumstances the arrest was not unlawful and the arrest was held to have taken place at 7.00 a.m.

Although *Murray* could be termed a 'terrorist' case, there is no legal justification for drawing a distinction on that ground. The judiciary gives greater consideration for crime control principles here.

Although the *Murray* case did not involve s. 28, if the same approach is taken in respect of s. 28 by the judiciary it gives greater consideration for crime control principles here. This would be interesting as the rules in the context of s. 28 of PACE 1984 appears to be mandatory.

Conclusion

It may be said that the existing powers conferred by PACE 1984 underline crime control values. Although the Royal Commission on Criminal Procedure viewed arrest as intrinsically coercive and wanted to restrict it to situations where it was necessary, s. 24 does not impose such a requirement.

Although the passage quoted in the question suggests that the innocent have nothing to fear, the extensive arrest powers can result in individual liberties being infringed when arrest is unnecessary. It may be unworkable to insist on tighter definitions of 'reasonable suspicion'. Instead what can be done is greater use of the summons procedure as the Royal Commission on Criminal Procedure recommended. One cannot expect the police to be trusted with wide arrest powers without making mistakes. The police it can be said virtually operate according to their own priorities in view of their powers to arrest for breach of the peace and other public order offences.

QUESTION 3

'Rights of suspects stop at the door of the police station.' Discuss.

Commentary

The question requires you not only to examine the rights of suspects when arrested, but also the area of search and seizure, and rights when in custody. It is necessary to state a view on the issue of the rights of suspects as to whether the rights do stop at the door of the police station.

Suggested Answer

The quotation proceeds on the basis that suspects are better protected outside the police station than inside. In order to consider such an assessment it is necessary first to consider how the Police and Criminal Evidence Act 1984 deals with the rights of suspects outside the police station.

PACE 1984 attempts to strike a balance between the due process model and the crime prevention or crime control model. The police can only arrest a suspect without a warrant if there is some justification which is either that an arrestable offence is being committed or the constable reasonably believes that an arrestable offence is about to be committed. Section 24 also enables a constable to justify arrest if he or she reasonably believes that an arrestable offence has been committed and the suspect was guilty of the offence.

The provisions in s. 24 ensure that the coercive power of an arrest is only to be utilised in relation to 'arrestable offences' thus ensuring that it is only used where it is needed for the purposes of prosecution.

An 'arrestable offence', by s. 24(1), is an offence for which the sentence is fixed by law or the maximum prison term for which a person of 21 years or over if convicted may be imprisoned is at least five years. Thus these are the type of offences that are normally more serious. Section 24(2) also makes arrestable certain offences contrary to the Official Secrets Acts 1911 to 1989, offences under the customs and excise legislation and offences relating to prostitution.

In the case of other offences which are not arrestable, arrest can only be effected without a warrant where certain arrest conditions apply. These conditions contained in s. 25 only allow the coercive power of arrest to be effected where a constable is unable to establish a suspect's identity or there is a need to protect the arrested person or property or there is some obstruction to the highway or an offence against public decency.

Section 28 requires a constable making an arrest to inform the suspect of the grounds of arrest. If this is not complied with then the arrest would be unlawful. Here the due process requirements would ensure that a citizen's rights are not unnecessarily violated. In dealing with the issue of due process in relation to the general arrest conditions, in *G* v *Director of Public Prosecutions* [1989] Crim LR 150, the Divisional Court, in reviewing the legality of an arrest under s. 25, was prepared to accept the constable's view that a person arrested committing an offence would not give his or her real name and address. It is submitted that the constable did not provide reasons that can be justified objectively as the words 'reasonable grounds for doubting' in s. 25(3)(c) require.

A constable can, under s. 32, search a suspect if the constable has grounds for believing that the person may harm him- or herself or others. A constable can also search a person to obtain evidence in relation to an offence for which the person was arrested. Section 32(3) is a due process requirement which ensures that the power of search is only exercised when it is reasonably necessary.

It is necessary now to consider the position when the suspect is taken to the police station. The main concern at this stage is with the treatment and manner of questioning of the suspect as the police would be concerned with obtaining confessions. The Royal Commission on Criminal Procedure was well aware of oppressive and persuasive tactics to obtain confessions. The crime control system surfaces a great deal at this stage as the interview in police custody may proceed on the basis that the suspect is guilty and the constraints of the law of evidence place pressure on the police to obtain confessions.

PACE 1984 together with the Codes of Practice issued under s. 66 of the Act ensure that the suspect is not subject to any oppression and that interviews should be tape recorded or, if this is not possible, accurately recorded in writing. The Codes of Practice and s. 58 of PACE refer to access to a solicitor when the suspect is in custody. These provisions are affected by changes brought in by the Criminal Justice and Public Order Act 1994 which encourage a suspect to speak. The caution indicates to the suspect that if questions are not answered during an interview an adverse inference may be drawn at trial.

The other problem here is the manner in which trial judges deal with breaches of the Codes of Practice by the police. The courts have taken the approach illustrated by *R v Keenan* [1990] 2 QB 54 that only 'substantial' breaches of the Codes justify exclusion of evidence under PACE 1984, s. 78 (which allows the court to exclude any admissible evidence which the prosecution were to rely on if the admission of the evidence would have an adverse effect on the fairness of the proceedings). The courts do not see their function as punishing the police by excluding evidence where there are breaches of PACE 1984 or the Codes. In *R v Mason* [1988] 1 WLR 139, the defendant was charged with arson and at the police station was deliberately misled by the police when they told him that they had found his fingerprints on what was said to be a fragment of a glass container containing the flammable liquid used in the arson. The police had also misled the solicitor who was present at the police station to provide advice to the defendant. The defendant then made a confession admitting the offence. The Court of Appeal held that the confession was inadmissible as, although the confession was voluntary, the deception particularly practised on the solicitor had an adverse effect on the fairness of the proceedings. It seems that a different view would have been taken if the deception had been practised on the defendant alone. It would be better for the law to permit a judge to exclude evidence where the conduct of the police brings the administration of justice into disrepute.

Inside a police station a suspect will be questioned. The Royal Commission on Criminal Justice found that the object of police questioning was to 'exploit vulnerabilities in ''ordinary'' people'. Questions are often asked in the form of statements such as, 'You did it. You were there.'

Questions are stated so that legally the defendant is going to be bound by the answer, for example, 'So you stole the goods?'

It would appear that despite the safeguards introduced by PACE 1984 and the Codes of Practice it would not be possible to have any effect on police interrogation techniques and this would continue to be the case so long as the police follow an adversarial system.

Conclusion

It may be said that a suspect's rights are curtailed when he or she arrives at the police station. What is probably needed is a requirement that a trial judge issue a warning to the jury on the unreliability of convicting purely on a confession. This was a recommendation of the Royal Commission on Criminal Justice but the government has not acted on it.

Some safeguards were introduced under PACE 1984 such as the right to legal advice in the police station and the tape recording of interviews. However, these really do not produce an adequate balance to the police powers as described above.

QUESTION 4

Evaluate the discretion that a court has to exclude admissible evidence under s. 78 of the Police and Criminal Evidence Act 1984. Consider whether s. 78 provides an adequate balance in ensuring that the police comply with the Act and the relevant Codes of Practice.

Commentary

The question requires first a consideration of the exclusionary discretion that judges possess at common law in dealing with prejudicial evidence. The answer should concentrate on the existence of s. 78 as an additional discretion particularly to deal with PACE 1984 and the Codes of Practice. There should be focus here on how the courts have interpreted their powers under s. 78 in a restrictive manner since they are concerned with fairness in terms of maintaining a balance between the prosecution and the defence.

Suggested Answer

In criminal cases a trial judge has a discretion at common law to exclude evidence which is otherwise admissible on the ground that such probative value is substantially outweighed by its prejudicial effect.

The exclusionary discretion is given statutory force in s. 78(1) of PACE 1984 which provides:

> In any proceedings the court may refuse to allow evidence on which the prosecution proposes to rely to be given if it appears to the court that, having regard to all the circumstances, including the circumstanes in which the evidence was obtained, the admission of the evidence would have such an adverse effect on the fairness of the proceedings that the court ought not to admit it.

The provisions of s. 78 are different from the common law as the section expressly provides that the circumstances in which the evidence was obtained may be taken into account in assessing whether the admission of the evidence would have an adverse effect on the fairness of the proceedings. Prior to s. 78 the House of Lords had held in *R* v *Sang* [1980] AC 402 that the manner in which evidence was obtained could be considered only if it was confession evidence. Otherwise, even if evidence was improperly or illegally obtained it would be admissible so long as it was relevant.

The other way in which s. 78 differs from the common law is its reference to fairness as a criterion as opposed to bad faith, oppression or deception. The working of s. 78 may be assessed by considering its use in cases where there has been wrongful exclusion of legal advice contrary to s. 58 of PACE 1984 and the Codes of Practice.

In *R* v *Alladice* (1988) 87 Cr App R 380, the Court of Appeal held that even in the absence of bad faith, a trial judge must consider whether possible unfairness requires the exclusion of a confession if the defendant has improperly been denied access to a solicitor in breach of PACE 1984, s. 58. The Court of Appeal also emphasised that the trial judge would have to consider the background of the suspect and to what extent legal advice would have made a difference as regards the obtaining of the confession. The emphasis, as can be seen in *R* v *Alladice*, is on the unfairness.

The point can be seen in the case of *R* v *Quinn* [1990] Crim LR 581. Here the prosecution relied on visual identification through a procedure which was carried out abroad. Lord Lane CJ said that the function of the judge was to protect the fairness of the proceedings, but if proceedings became unfair, for example, because of abuse of process, then the evidence would be inadmissible. In *R* v *Quinn* the Court of Appeal was not prepared to interfere as the trial judge had taken the relevant factors into account. Trial judges thus have a wide discretion and this would also depend on the facts. The Court of Appeal has stated that it is not the function of the courts to deal with police discipline and so prosecution evidence should not be excluded purely to punish the police for breaches of the Codes of Practice or PACE 1984.

As for the part of the Codes that relate to the questioning of suspects, the approach of the courts has been to consider whether breaches have been 'flagrant' or 'deliberate'. In *R* v *Canale* [1990] 2 All ER 187, the police officers questioning the suspects had ignored the part of Code C that required questions and answers to be recorded contemporaneously. The officers stated that it was the 'best way' to deal with the situation. The Court of Appeal in *R* v *Canale* was concerned with the fact that the police had acted as if PACE 1984 and the Codes did not exist. The decision in *R* v *Canale* also emphasises what the Court of Appeal had stated in the earlier case of *R* v *Keenan* [1990] 2 QB 54. That was a case where the police had also not recorded questions and answers to an interview in the form of an interview record. The court stated that the Codes must be taken seriously and that trial judges should not be slow to exclude where 'substantial' breaches have occurred.

The cases also show that there is a tendency for evidence to be excluded not only where there has been a particular breach of the Codes of Practice, but also where there has been manifest unfairness.

In *R* v *Mason* [1988] 1 WLR 139, the defendant was charged with arson, and the prosecution only had the confession evidence of the defendant which they had only obtained after practising a deception on the defendant and his solicitor. The police had misled the defendant and the solicitor into thinking that the defendant's fingerprints were on a fragment of glass claimed to be from a container which had held flammable liquid. The Court of Appeal was prepared to exclude the confession even though it was reliable and had been obtained without oppression. It was the deception, particularly on the solicitor who was also an officer of the court, that seems to have influenced the court in exercising the discretion under s. 78. The Court of Appeal hoped that such practices would not occur. *R* v *Mason* could have been decided in the same way under the common law because of the deception practised by the police.

Another area that may be considered is entrapment. According to the Court of Appeal in *R* v *Smurthwaite* [1994] 1 All ER 898, when considering whether to exclude evidence obtained by entrapment a trial judge should consider whether it consists of admissions to a completed offence or relates to the actual commission of an offence, and whether there is an unassailable record.

The approach of the courts has been to insist on strict adherence to Code of Practice C in relation to cautioning and the proper maintaining of interview records only when the suspect is vulnerable to abuse or pressure. In *R* v *Christou* [1992] QB 979, the accused had been recorded on tape and video talking to undercover officers. The Court of Appeal treated the accused and the police as being on an equal footing so that the fact that the accused had not been cautioned did not make it unfair to admit the evidence.

In *R* v *Bailey* [1993] 3 All ER 513, the police were permitted to rely on a conversation between co-accused that had taken place in a bugged cell even when the defendants had exercised their right of silence at an interview. The Court of Appeal held that Code C did not prohibit the bugging of cells. It would appear that the court is concerned with the probative force of the evidence and would permit evidence to be admitted so long as the unfairness is not manifest at the trial.

Conclusion

The decisions of the courts do not deter the police from breaching the Codes of Practice. In the case of entrapment and methods such as secret recording devices, the courts in their decisions have the effect of encouraging such behaviour. However, on balance s. 78 is better than the earlier common law as it expressly permits a court to take into account all the circumstances including how the evidence was obtained. In this sense the section takes a middle ground since evidence is not automatically excluded merely because of the manner in which it was obtained.

11   Problem Questions on Police Powers

INTRODUCTION

This chapter deals with problem-type questions concerning police powers.

In relation to powers of arrest, it should be realised that arrest without a warrant is covered by the Police and Criminal Evidence Act 1984 (PACE 1984). Arrests are governed by the 'necessity' principle advocated by the Royal Commission on Criminal Procedure, which is given effect in ss. 24 and 25 of PACE 1984. Essentially the Royal Commission on Criminal Procedure was attempting to balance due process considerations with crime control principles.

On the topic of searches the relevant provisions in PACE 1984 attempt to balance due process with crime control considerations by ensuring that the police have sufficient powers to enter premises and search if someone has been lawfully arrested and it is reasonably suspected that evidence is to be found on the premises.

When attempting exam questions in this area it is essential to consider the appropriate remedies under civil law, such as false imprisonment and assault.

In relation to treatment of persons in custody, PACE 1984 again attempts to balance crime control and due process considerations. The provisions give the police considerable powers and at the same time provide checks and controls on the use of those powers and provide safeguards for suspects.

QUESTION 1

(a) On the night of 15 November last while walking past No. 16 Acacia Avenue, Norman heard a noise of breaking glass. On turning round he saw a figure of what looked like a man running past him. Norman chased him and brought the man down, and later got another passer-by to call the police. The police took the man to the police station. It has since been discovered that the man, Blackburn, was out jogging and wore black as it was his favourite colour and was not guilty of any offence. No one in Acacia Avenue has reported a burglary or damage to property on 15 November. Advise Blackburn who is considering an action against the police and/or Norman.

(b) PC Bright was on foot patrol when he saw Harriet riding her bike without lights. PC Bright had previously arrested Harriet for the theft of bikes. He ran after her, held her bike and forced her off it. He told her that she was 'nicked' and questioned her about the bike. He then took her to her house where he questioned her for a further eight hours. Harriet has now been informed that she is not going to be charged with any offences. Assess the legality of PC Bright's conduct.

Commentary

Part **(a)** of the question requires a consideration of s. 24(5) and (6) of the Police and Criminal Evidence Act 1984. In the beginning of the answer it would be necessary to identify the cause of action that is available to Blackburn.

Part **(b)** is concerned with PACE 1984, s. 24(6), and related powers of arrest. It is also necessary to consider police powers in relation to questioning and custody.

Suggested Answer

(a) The cause of action that Blackburn would want to pursue here is an action in damages for false imprisonment. The possible claims are against the police force and Norman. It is necessary to start first with the position of Norman.

Claim against Norman

Norman used force and restricted Blackburn's liberty for a period of time. Blackburn would only be able to justify the arrest if PACE 1984, s. 24(5), applied.

By s. 24(5), when an arrestable offence has been committed any person may arrest without a warrant (a) anyone who is guilty of the offence or (b) anyone whom he suspects on reasonable grounds to be guilty of it. On the facts of this question, Norman would be able to show that when he proceeded to chase and later arrest Blackburn there were reasonable grounds for suspecting that a burglary had been committed. There was the noise of breaking glass, and he spotted Blackburn running past him, which would help to establish grounds to believe that it was Blackburn who was guilty of an offence. The difficulty that Norman would face is that s. 24(5) gives a power of arrest only if an arrestable offence has actually been committed. There would seem to be no possibility of Norman showing that an arrestable offence has been committed to which Blackburn could be connected. The position under PACE 1984, s. 24(5) is similar to the common law before the Act. In *Walters* v *W. H. Smith and Son Ltd* [1914] 1 KB 595, a store detective arrested a person for theft. However, no offence had been committed and the arrest was unlawful despite the fact that there did seem to be grounds for suspecting that the person arrested had committed an offence. The reasoning in *Walters* was applied in *R* v *Self* (1992) 1 WLR 692 when interpreting s. 24(5). The wording of s. 24(5) would mean that any arrest by an individual other than a police constable would be unlawful if an offence has not been committed. Therefore Blackburn would be able successfully to claim damages for his false imprisonment.

Claim against the Police

In order to consider if the arrest by the police was unlawful it is necessary to consider s. 24(6) of PACE 1984. By this section so long as the constable reasonably suspects that an individual has committed an arrestable offence it does not matter that such an offence has not been committed. By the time the police arrived, there were circumstances to show that an offence had been committed. Any constable would be able to show, as required by s. 24(6), that there were reasonable grounds to suspect that an arrestable offence had been committed. These circumstances would be provided mainly by Norman's account of how he came to arrest Blackburn.

There is a contrast here with s. 24(5), as even if it has now been found that no arrestable offence was committed the arrest by the police would be lawful.

In the circumstances the police would not be liable for damages. It is assumed for the purposes of the answer that the police have complied with the requirement in s. 28 of PACE 1984 to provide information to Blackburn of the grounds for his arrest.

(b)   It is necessary first to consider the issue of arrest and whether PC Bright exercised his powers of arrest lawfully.

Was there an Arrest?

Holding Harriet's bike and forcing her off it constitute arrest.

There is no definition of arrest in PACE 1984 but at common law any deprivation of liberty can be an arrest. PC Bright would want to claim that he had reasonable grounds to believe that Harriet had committed theft and that therefore he had grounds to suspect that an arrestable offence had been committed and that she is guilty of such an offence.

It is important to remember that PC Bright is only going on what he knows about Harriet, and not necessarily on other evidence.

Turning to the guidance given by the courts about what is reasonable suspicion, in the House of Lords' decision of *Hussien* v *Chong Fook Kam* [1970] AC 942, Lord Devlin pointed out that prima facie proof consists of admissible evidence. This would suggest that mere suspicion or a hunch would not be sufficient. In *Dumbell* v *Roberts* [1944] 1 All ER 326, Scott LJ said that the police should act on the assumption that their prima facie suspicion may be ill-founded. In the Code of Practice issued by the Home Office in respect of the stop and search powers, the guidance states that there must be an objective basis for reasonable suspicion, which cannot be based only on personal factors such as age, colour, hairstyle or knowledge of a relevant conviction.

Assuming that PC Bright is able to justify the arrest on the basis of s. 24(6), that he has grounds to suspect that Harriet has committed the offence, it is necessary to consider s. 28.

PACE 1984, Section 28

PACE 1984, s. 28, requires a constable who makes an arrest to inform the arrested person of the fact of, and reasons for, arrest either immediately or as soon as practicable afterwards.

In *Abbassy* v *Commissioner of Police of the Metropolis* [1990] 1 WLR 385, the Court of Appeal followed the earlier House of Lords' decision of *Christie* v *Leachinsky* [1947] AC 573, in which it was held that precise or technical language need not be used provided the substance of the offence is brought to the attention of the person who is arrested.

According to the statement of facts in the question, PC Bright did not make any reference to the substance of an offence when telling Harriet she was 'nicked'. Harriet's arrest was therefore unlawful all the way up to the time the proper reason was given.

PACE 1984, Section 30

PACE 1984, s. 30, requires persons who have been arrested other than in a police station to be taken to a police station, which should be a designated police station. This is to ensure that the safeguards in the Act in relation to police detention can apply.

PC Bright took Harriet to her home, but this can only be done pursuant to s. 30(10) if it is necessary to carry out investigations that it is reasonable to carry out immediately.

The breach of s. 30 would only constitute a breach of a statutory duty and would not necessarily in any way reflect upon the arrest.

QUESTION 2

While on patrol, PC Dixon encountered the following incidents:

(a)   On a busy road he found a man lying down to protest against traffic congestion and since there was a danger of injury, he forced the man off the road and arrested him.

(b)   He spotted a driver not stopping at a traffic light and signalled the driver to stop. The driver stopped but did not have his driver's licence and when asked his address and name gave answers that PC Dixon believed were not true. Dixon arrested the driver.

(c)   PC Dixon saw a man about to snatch the shopping bag of an elderly woman. Dixon effected an arrest by applying an armlock and in the process fractured the man's arm.

(d)   PC Dixon came across a man who he knew had previous convictions in relation to burglary. Dixon was also aware that there were burglaries in the area. When he stopped the man to question him about the burglaries, Dixon found that the man was not cooperative. He asked the man to come with him. The man refused and Dixon arrested him.

You are asked to advise PC Dixon on the legal position.

Commentary

Parts (a) and (b) deal with the general conditions of arrest contained in s. 25 of the Police and Criminal Evidence Act 1984. In part (c) the question deals with the use of force in effecting an arrest. Part (d) deals with whether the police can arrest for the purposes of questioning.

Suggested Answer

(a)   PC Dixon here would be concerned with the general powers of arrest in PACE 1984, s. 25. This provision permits the arrest of persons even though there is no offence that is an arrestable one.

The object of s. 25 is to widen powers of arrest without a warrant to cover all offences, provided that one of the general arrest conditions is satisfied. In part (a) of the question, PC Dixon was concerned about the risk of injury to the man while he remained on the busy road. This would satisfy the condition in s. 25(3)(d)(ii) that the 'relevant person' could suffer physical injury and that PC Dixon reasonably believed that the arrest was necessary to prevent such injury.

It is also necessary for PC Dixon to show that the relevant person has committed an offence, which would be obstruction of the highway, and the power of arrest here can be exercised even if the offence is not an arrestable one, so long as the condition in s. 25(3)(d)(ii) is satisfied. PC Dixon could also justify the arrest pursuant to s. 25(3)(d)(v) that the man was causing an unlawful obstruction to the highway.

(b)   Here again one is concerned with the application of the general arrest conditions. On the facts in this part of the question although the traffic offence committed by the driver is not an arrestable offence, by s. 25(3) if one of the general arrest conditions is satisfied the arrest can be justified.

On stopping the driver, PC Dixon found that the particulars the driver furnished were not true. To justify an arrest, PC Dixon has to show that he had reasonable grounds for doubting the correctness of the name (s. 25(3)(b)) and/or address (s. 25(3)(c)). It is not clear what PC Dixon's reasons for suspecting the answers are. It must be shown objectively that there were reasons for doubting the answers.

It could be argued that, as PC Dixon disbelieved the name the driver gave, the driver's name was unknown to and could not be ascertained by PC Dixon so that arrest was justified under s. 25(3)(a). However, this would have to be abandoned if the name turned out to be correct, for then it would have been known to Dixon at the time of the arrest.

(c)   PC Dixon would be able to justify the arrest on the basis of s. 24(4) as he saw the person committing an arrestable offence. The main concern here is going to be with the use of force. A person making an arrest may, by s. 3 of the Criminal Law Act 1967, use reasonable force against the person arrested. In determining whether force is reasonable, the courts have indicated that it is necessary to take into account the resistance to arrest, the seriousness of the offence which led to the arrest, and the nature and degree of risk which making the arrest poses to third parties.

Here it could be argued that the use of handcuffs would have been reasonable force but that the application of the armlock was excessive. PC Dixon could be liable for damages for the battery.

(d)   The issue here is the power of police officers to ask individual questions. At common law an individual who does not answer questions is free to walk off. The common law ensures that individuals are free to go about their own business unless they have been arrested.

On the facts it does not appear that PC Dixon effected any arrest when he approached the man to question him. PC Dixon was entitled to ask questions on the basis of seeking cooperation.

However, when the man refused to answer questions, PC Dixon was not in any position to effect an arrest.

In *Rice* v *Connolly* [1966] 2 QB 414, officers on the beat came across a Mr Rice. They proceeded to ask questions about burglaries in the area and he was asked to account for his movements. When the man answered only some questions and the policemen wanted the man to accompany them, he refused and was arrested for wilfully obstructing the officers. The court held that Mr Rice was not obstructing and the arrest was unlawful.

On the facts here the position would be the same and the man would have a cause of action against the police for false imprisonment.

QUESTION 3

Danny works part-time framing paintings. Last night he was carrying a painting home after having collected it from the owner. It was late at night and as Danny was about to reach his garden gate PC Pigg stopped Danny and asked what he was doing and following Danny's explanation Pigg insisted on taking Danny's key to the house and carried out a search.

PC Pigg found a railway sign which Danny had stolen many years ago. Danny was taken back to the police station and charged with theft of the railway sign.

Advise Danny.

Commentary

This question's main focus is on the powers of search and seizure but it also involves some aspects of powers of arrest without warrant. This would involve the Police and Criminal Evidence Act 1984, ss. 18 and 19.

Suggested Answer

It would be necessary to start with PC Pigg's entry on to the premises. It is clear on the facts that Danny had not in any way invited PC Pigg into his house and this would make PC Pigg and the relevant chief constable of the police force liable in damages for trespass. The only way PC Pigg could avoid liability is to justify entering the premises under s. 18 of the Police and Criminal Evidence Act 1984.

Police and Criminal Evidence Act 1984, Section 18

By s. 18(1) of PACE 1984, PC Pigg can justify entry upon the premises if there has been an arrest for an arrestable offence and he had reasonable grounds for suspecting that the premises contain evidence or other items relating to the offence.

On the facts there does not seem to be any evidence of an arrest. Danny was answering PC Pigg's questions about the painting he was carrying, which suggests that he was cooperating and was not in any way told that he was under arrest. If there was an arrest, PC Pigg should have complied with the requirements of s. 28 of PACE 1984.

It could be assumed that when PC Pigg took Danny's keys from him there was no arrest of Danny for an arrestable offence.

Seizure of the Railway Sign

Danny is going to be concerned with whether the seizure of the sign is lawful. If it is not lawful then there is the issue of whether the railway sign can be utilised in evidence against him.

By s. 19 of PACE 1984, there is a general power conferred on a police constable to seize property while on premises. This power of seizure can only be exercised if the constable is lawfully on the premises.

The power of seizure can be utilised if the constable finds that there is evidence of some other crime other than the one for which he has effected an arrest and it is necessary to preserve the evidence.

On the facts it would appear that the seizure of the railway sign is illegal as PC Pigg cannot justify his initial entry on the premises.

Use of the Railway Sign in Evidence

The position in English Law generally is that so long as the evidence is relevant and is admissible the manner in which it is obtained is irrelevant.

However, by s. 78 of the Police and Criminal Evidence Act 1984 the trial judge has a discretion to exclude evidence if admitting it, in all the circumstances, including the manner in which it was obtained, would have an adverse effect on the fairness of the proceedings.

It could be argued here that the evidence of the railway sign is admissible as all Danny can complain of is the manner of PC Pigg entering upon the premises and there is no other way the admissibility of the sign would have an adverse effect on the fairness of the proceedings.

QUESTION 4

Jacko was arrested by PC Boot on a charge of burglary. The arrest was lawful and Jacko was taken to the Sunhill Police Station. At the station the custody officer, Sergeant Bill, refused Jacko the opportunity to consult his solicitor.

Jacko was questioned non-stop for 24 hours with teams of police officers asking the same questions as the investigating officer. They were keen to obtain a confession. At the end of the period of 24 hours Jacko, who was tired, hungry and thirsty, decided finally to confess. Discuss the lawfulness of the conduct of the police.

Commentary

The question deals with the provisions of the Police and Criminal Evidence Act 1984 dealing with custody, treatment of persons in detention and access to legal advice. There is also a need to consider the provisions relating to confessions. It would be necessary to discuss Code of Practice C issued pursuant to PACE 1984.

Suggested Answer

It is stated in the question that the arrest was lawful. What has to be considered is the rights of a person who has been brought to a police station. The station here is a designated station as the facts indicate that there is a custody officer.

Duties of the Custody Officer

A custody officer should be at least of the rank of sergeant. PACE 1984 requires the custody officer to ensure that a custody record is maintained, recording everything that takes place in relation to the suspect. The custody officer has to advise the suspect of rights to consult a solicitor in private, and if the suspect does not request to consult a solicitor of his or her choice then the custody officer must arrange for a duty solicitor to be made available, if there is a duty solicitor scheme in operation.

By s. 58 of PACE 1984, the custody officer must permit access to a solicitor unless an officer of at least the rank of superintendent authorises a delay of access to a solicitor.

From the facts stated in the question it would appear that it was the custody officer, Sergeant Bill, who took the decision to deny access to a solicitor. This would be a breach of s. 58. By s. 58(8) the relevant officer can delay access only if he or she reasonably believes that a serious arrestable offence has been committed and that denying access is necessary because access would lead to interference with, or harm to, evidence connected with a serious arrestable offence or interference with, or injury to, persons or that others who are not arrested would be alerted, or there would be interference with the recovery of any property obtained as a result of a serious arrestable offence.

In *R* v *Samuel* [1988] QB 615, the Court of Appeal held that the right to legal advice is a fundamental right.

Detention and Treatment of Persons in Custody

PACE 1984 provides a framework whereby a decision has to be taken at various stages whether detention has to continue, or whether there should be release on bail.

By s. 40, after the first six hours and every nine hours thereafter there must be reviews of detention which are the responsibility of the custody officer.

At the end of 24 hours an officer of the rank of superintendent must decide whether detention without charge is to continue. Detention without charge can only be justified if the relevant officer is satisfied that the investigations are being carried out diligently and that evidence can be obtained through questioning or that detention is necessary to preserve evidence. On the facts of the question the detention without charge was carried out by the investigation officer purely for the purposes of obtaining a confession. This would not be possible under PACE 1984.

There is also the issue of the treatment of Jacko in custody. The Codes of Practice dealing with treatment and questioning of persons require that there be appropriate breaks between questioning and an opportunity for sleep.

Admissibility of the Confession

PACE 1984, s. 76(2), provides that a confession relied upon by the prosecution cannot be admitted in evidence unless the prosecution show that it was not obtained by oppression of the person who made it or in consequence of anything said or done which was likely, in the circumstances existing at the time, to render unreliable any confession.

In *R* v *Fulling* [1987] QB 426, it was held that the word 'oppression' has its dictionary meaning, that is, the exercise of power or authority in a burdensome, harsh or wrongful manner.

Here the confession had been obtained when Jacko broke down after repeated questioning for 24 hours by the police. Asking the same questions deliberately for 24 hours would constitute oppression. In *R* v *Miller* (1992) *The Times*, 24 December 1992, being asked the same question over 300 times was held to amount to oppression. A tape recording of this was played to the Court of Appeal and their lordships were of the view that they could hear the person breaking down. In such circumstances the confession would be excluded pursuant to s. 76(2).

Breaches of the provisions of PACE 1984 and the Codes of Practice can lead to disciplinary proceedings against the relevant officers.

QUESTION 5

Y, a uniformed police constable, saw X walking down a street just after midnight carrying a big bag. Many burglaries had taken place in this area over the past few weeks. Y went to stop X to ask him what was in the bag and asked to search X's pockets. X continued walking. Y then put his hand on X's arm. X turned and pushed Y away. Y fell to the ground. Y called for assistance. X was taken to the police station where he was straight away locked up in a cell and left there for over two hours before being questioned. The questioning was first carried out by Z and then by Z and A. X was in fact a shift worker returning home. He had gone to work for the night shift but had not been feeling too well because he had a headache and so had left work early. He was in a bad uncommunicative mood because of the headache and was rushing home to take some medication for it. X is very upset and seeks your advice.

Commentary

This question highlights the lack of remedies when someone is wrongly arrested. Even though one could argue that X should have been more cooperative and perhaps if he had then he would not have suffered what happened it has to be remembered that unless a police officer can invoke the powers contained in PACE 1984 a citizen has no obligation to cooperate.

Suggested Answer

Y, a uniformed police officer, wanted to know what was in X's bag and pockets. By PACE 1984, s. 1, a police officer can only stop and search somebody if the officer has reasonable grounds for suspecting that stolen or prohibited articles will be found. Relevant prohibited articles would be those that would assist in carrying out burglaries as these are the offences that have been committed in the area in the past few weeks.

A police constable who has such reasonable grounds can carry out the search before carrying out the arrest. However, by s. 2(3), before carrying out the search, the police officer must take reasonable steps to give his or her name and the name of the police station to which he or she is attached, to state the object of the proposed search, and the constable's grounds for proposing to make it. Further a constable cannot require a person to remove any of his clothing in public other than an outer coat, jacket or gloves. Here the constable wants to look at what is in the pockets which is part of the outer clothing.

If a person consents to being stopped and searched then there is no need for the police officer to comply with ss. 1 and 2. However, it is very clear on the facts of this question that X is not consenting and is actually resisting. Therefore Y will have to comply with the requirements of ss. 1 and 2.

The question that has to be considered is whether there were 'reasonable grounds for suspecting' that stolen or prohibited articles would be found. The facts indicate that X is walking through an area where there have been a lot of burglaries in recent weeks, it is late at night when most burglaries take place, he is a man walking alone and most burglaries are by men and he has a big bag which could contain the proceeds of a burglary and the implements to carry out such a burglary such as a jemmy. Equally it could contain the ordinary belongings of X.

The Privy Council in *Hussien* v *Chong Fook Kam* [1970] AC 942 indicated that reasonable cause, which has the same meaning as reasonable suspicion, meant a lower standard than information sufficient to prove a prima facie case. Suspicion arises at or near the starting point of an investigation. The obtaining of prima facie proof is an end. Prima facie proof consists of admissible evidence. Suspicion can take into account matters that could not be put in evidence at all.

It may be that a person's refusal to stop when asked to do so by a police officer can add to the officer's reasonable grounds. Y stopped X solely because he already suspected, but X's reaction might transform this into a reasonable suspicion. However, the reasonable suspicion test is vague.

Once the reasonable suspicion test is satisfied then by s. 1(2)(b) the police officer has the power to detain a person for a search. Police officers may question any persons they wish prior to detention or arrest but there is no obligation to answer these questions. Suspects must submit to search and detention but they need not answer questions.

If the search of X was not legally permissible because of non-compliance with the requirements of PACE 1984 then X will want to know if he has any remedies. A search was not actually carried out at the time of the stop.

PACE 1984 itself does not make it a crime or a tort to stop and search someone unlawfully or to fail to provide information before search or to fail to make a record of it afterwards. However, at common law a failure to provide information prior to search renders the stop and search unlawful. It was held in *Pedro v Diss* [1981] 2 All ER 59, which followed *Christie v Leachinsky* [1947] AC 573, that detention was unlawful if the reason for it was not provided. In *Pedro v Diss* the suspect was charged with assaulting a police officer in the execution of his duty after the defendant used force to free himself from detention. The unlawfulness of the detention meant that the police officer was not acting in the execution of his duty and so the assault was not criminal.

However, PACE 1984, s. 2(2), states that a police officer has to take reasonable steps to provide requisite information to the person whom he wants to stop and search. It can be argued that Y could not do this because of X's reaction. If it was X's own fault that he did not receive the information then it is arguable that this should not make the stop unlawful if there was reasonable suspicion to justify the stop in the first place.

However, here it is arguable that the stop and search was unlawful because either the requisite information was not given or because there was no reasonable suspicion.

It is only if the stop was unlawful that X could have behaved in the way he did without incurring criminal liability for assault. *Rice v Connolly* [1966] 2 QB 414 is authority for the proposition that refusal to go to a police station and answer police officers' questions is not obstructing the police officers in the execution of their duty and that a person does not have to go to a police station unless arrested.

However, the courts have taken the approach that whilst citizens are entitled not to answer questions, officers are entitled to ask them to cooperate. The courts have permitted an officer to attract the attention of a person in order to ask questions. In *Donnelly v Jackman* [1970] 1 WLR 562, a police officer tapped a man on the shoulder so as to speak to him about an offence. The man turned round and tapped the officer on the chest. The officer again tapped the man on the shoulder, the man then hit the officer. This was held to be an assault on an officer in the execution of his duty. The court held that the officer's tapping of the shoulder was 'a trivial interference' with a citizen's liberty. The triviality of this interference did not take the officer beyond his duty. However, *Donnelly* v *Jackman* has to be considered with *Bentley* v *Brudzinski* (1982) 75 Cr App R 217, in which an officer stopped and questioned two men who fitted the general description of people allegedly involved in the taking away of a car without consent. Another officer arrived who wished to question the men. They were moving away and so the officer placed his hand on the shoulder of one them and was then punched. The defendant was acquitted of assaulting an officer in the execution of his duty because the action of the officer was held to be outside his duty. Thus it will depend on the circumstances whether the interference is trivial or not.

Here Y put his hand on X's arm. It is arguable that this is only a trivial interference. Therefore it is arguable that X assaulted Y. Further the assault here amounts to assault occasioning actual bodily harm contrary to the Offences against the Person Act 1861, s. 47, which is an arrestable offence. Another offence that has been committed is assaulting a police officer in the execution of his duty contrary to the Police Act 1964, s. 51. This is not an arrestable offence but it is possible to arrest pursuant to PACE 1984, s. 25, where a person is causing physical injury to somebody else and the police officer wants to stop that.

X was then taken to the police station. As his liberty has been restrained this would amount to an arrest. However, he was not told why he was being arrested, whether it was because he was a suspect for the burglaries or because of the assault on PC Y.

PACE 1984, s. 28, requires certain information to be given on arrest. This information has to be given even though the fact of arrest is obvious. The arrest is not lawful unless the person arrested is informed that he or she is under arrest and what the grounds for arrest are as soon as is practicable after arrest.

At the time of arrest of X it can be argued that it was not practical to tell him of the arrest because of the assault. However, he should have been told as soon as was practical at least on arrival at the police station but he was kept for over two hours before he was questioned.

There is the case of *Director of Public Prosecutions* v *Hawkins* [1988] 1 WLR 1166, which takes the approach that the moment an arrested person is subdued he can be informed and so the information should be given before the person is taken to the police station. In *Director of Public Prosecutions* v *Hawkins* there was a violent struggle by the arrested person which delayed the giving of reasons but they were not given when the person was subdued. The court held that it was reasonable not to give information until the violent conduct had stopped but at that point the reasons should have been given. As they were not given the arrest only became unlawful at that point. In *Lewis* v *Chief Constable of the South Wales Constabulary* [1991] 1 All ER 206, a case concerning an action for false imprisonment, the Court of Appeal held that arrests were unlawful until the reasons for the arrests were given and at that stage the arrests became lawful.

Here X was not prepared to cooperate with the police and there was a struggle. At that stage it would not be reasonable to tell X the reasons for his arrest but once assistance arrived and he was subdued he should have been told. Therefore until he was told about the reasons for the arrest it was unlawful. He was only questioned after two hours, and presumably at that time was told of the reasons for the arrest which then became lawful.

Therefore X would have an action for unlawful imprisonment from the time he was subdued to the time the questioning started if he was told at that stage why he was arrested.

12 Defending Suspects at the Police Station, the Right to Silence and Plea Bargaining

INTRODUCTION

Right to Silence

There are two aspects to the right to silence:

(a) the right not to answer the police's questions; and

(b) the right not to have to give evidence at trial.

In theory these rights are still there but in certain circumstances the Criminal Justice and Public Order Act 1994 permits adverse inferences to be made if these rights are exercised. Sometimes it is argued that the right to silence has been abolished. That is not quite correct but as Professor Murphy has written the right has become worthless. Further any benefits or advantages from exercising it have been abolished. In this chapter the right to silence will be described as having been 'limited'.

It is convenient to consider the changes brought in by the 1994 Act under the following heads:

(a) Failure of the accused to mention facts later relied upon in courts.

(b) Failure of the accused to account for objects, substances, marks and his or her presence at the scene of a crime.

(c)   The position of the defendant who fails to testify at trial.

It should be borne in mind at which of the various stages the issue of the right to silence can arise in the course of a criminal prosecution.

Also one should consider the government's justification for bringing about changes in the law and particularly if there are adequate safeguards provided for the person in custody.

Professor Murphy in his preface to *Murphy on Evidence*, 5th ed. (London Blackstone Press, 1995) talks about how there has been a culmination of two decades of subtle change during which the rights of the accused have gradually been eroded. Professor Murphy goes on to state concerning the changes in the Criminal Justice and Public Order Act 1944 that:

> The apologists (for the most part, well-meaning and concerned people) say, as apologists always do, that it is in a good cause, and that the reforms are limited. It is a seductive argument, and, if taken in isolation, a true one. It is only in observation of the big picture that its falsity is exposed. It is true that the accused still enjoys the right not to be compelled to give evidence, and the right to remain silent. It is also true that those rights are now effectively worthless. The apologists make it difficult for anyone to dispute what they say without being branded a friend of the criminal. Yet ... the law exists not only, or even primarily, for criminals, but for those accused of crime, who (at the time of writing) are presumed to be innocent until proven guilty, and are entitled to be judged by a jury of their peers.

Plea Bargaining

Section 48 of the Criminal Justice and Public Order Act 1994 will permit plea bargaining by the accused to influence the sentence received. By encouraging plea bargaining, this section could undermine the presumption of innocence. It is arguable that pressure will be brought to bear on an accused to admit to offences, even if innocent, so as to guarantee a minimal sentence, where the defence looks weak.

Section 48 is as follows:

> (1)   In determining what sentence to pass on an offender who has pleaded guilty to an offence in proceedings before that or another court a court shall take into account—

(a)   the stage in the proceedings for the offence at which the offender indicated his intention to plead guilty, and

(b)   the circumstances in which this indication was given.

(2)   If, as a result of taking into account any matter referred to in subsection (1) above, the court imposes a punishment on the offender which is less severe than the punishment it would otherwise have imposed, it shall state in open court that it has done so.

For those students who have to study the effectiveness of Royal Commissions and the mechanics of law reform this is an area where the Royal Commission has been criticised for making recommendations that might have the effect of increasing the number of convictions of innocent persons. It also highlights the difficulties that terms of reference for a Royal Commission can cause. The Royal Commission recommended a clearly articulated system of sentence discounts and that earlier pleas should attract higher discounts. The Royal Commission also recommended a form of sentence canvassing that would involve a judge. The judge would be able to indicate the highest sentence that would be imposed on the basis of the facts then assumed.

The Royal Commission also approved of the practice of charge bargaining. This takes place between prosecution and defence lawyers where the defendant offers to plead guilty to a lesser charge if the more serious charge is dropped. The Royal Commission recommended that charge bargaining should be introduced at the earliest opportunity.

The reason why the Royal Commission took the approach that it did was because its terms of reference stated that it was to examine the effectiveness of the criminal justice system in:

(a)   securing the conviction of those guilty of criminal offences and

(b)   the acquittal of those who are innocent

(c)   having regard to the efficient use of resources.

There was an implication that all three of these matters were to be given equal weight. As a result of regarding all three matters as being of equal concern the Royal Commission saw no problems in recommending changes to the criminal justice sytem which could have the effect of substantially increasing the likelihood of innocent persons being convicted.

QUESTION 1

Consider whether the right to silence is a necessary safeguard or an obstacle to justice.

Commentary

The right to silence has been severely limited by the Criminal Justice and Public Order Act 1994. The question asks for consideration of whether in principle this should have happened.

Suggested Answer

The abolition of the right to silence has been controversial because two Royal Commissions were in favour of retaining it. These were the Royal Commission on Criminal Procedure and a majority of the Royal Commission on Criminal Justice. They argued that it should be retained because vulnerable suspects would be in jeopardy and might incriminate themselves, and that this could lead to more miscarriages of justice. However, the Home Secretary accepted the minority view of the Royal Commission on Criminal Justice. Critics have described this change as the limitation of a vital and long-tried principle destroyed for short-term political advantage. In fact it has been argued that this is an example of the destructive force of party politics on the administration of the law.

There are many reasons why persons would want to keep silent. They might do so for the protection of their family or friends, from a sense of bewilderment, embarrassment or outrage, or they may come to a reasoned decision to wait until the allegations against them have been set out in detail and they have had the benefit of considered legal advice.

Many of the miscarriages of justice have taken place because of unreliable confessions that have been obtained in the police station. There is evidence from the miscarriages of justice cases that people confess even if they are not forced brutally to confess, for example, Judith Ward and Stepfan Kiszko. The Royal Commission on Criminal Justice realised that some people, even those who are not mentally ill or handicapped, will confess to offences they did not commit.

The Royal Commission commissioned research concerning the right to silence. The research results suggested that the right was only exercised in a minority of cases, that there was no proof that silence is used disproportionately by experienced criminals, that silence in the police station did not improve the defendant's chances of an acquittal, and that most of those who are silent in the police station either plead guilty later or are subsequently found guilty. The Royal Commission was concerned that more innocent people might be convicted and that there was a risk of more pressure being put on suspects in the police station. Limiting the right to silence may help convict the guilty, but it will also make it easier to convict the innocent. However, the Royal Commission came to the view that the experienced criminals who remained silent would continue to do so even if the law was changed. At their trial they would seek to justify their silence by saying that they had been advised by their solicitors to say nothing until the allegations against them had been fully disclosed.

The Lord Chief Justice, Lord Taylor of Gosforth, was in favour of limiting the right to silence with some modifications which were accepted by the government. He gave the Tom Sargant Memorial Lecture in 1994 and gave his reasons for supporting the change. He was of the view that when a defendant fails to testify at trial there is nothing unfair in the jury being told that it is open to them to draw a proper inference from the absence of any answer by the defendant. He felt that this was consistent with common sense. With regard to silence when arrested or in the police station the Lord Chief Justice gave examples of when it would be reasonable to give an answer and if no satisfactory answer is given for the appropriate inference to be made. The Criminal Justice and Public Order Act 1994, s. 34, allows proper inferences to be drawn where a defendant relies at a trial on a fact which he failed to mention when he was questioned under caution or charged. In Lord Taylor's view this is entirely reasonable. He gave an example concerning a defendant charged with being knowingly concerned in importation of cocaine. He is arrested at an airport where he has gone to meet a co-defendant charged as the courier. He says nothing to the police. At trial, his defence is that he had gone to meet someone he believed to be bringing in a silver wedding present for his parents from a relative abroad. Lord Taylor said: 'Surely that is a fact which an innocent man would reasonably have been expected to put forward. Instead, it emerges at a stage when no investigation can be made of the feasibility of the story.'

Section 36 permits a proper inference to be drawn if, when arrested, the defendant had any object in his possession or any substance or mark upon him or his clothes giving rise to a reasonable belief that it is attributable to his involvement in the offence specified and the defendant fails to account for its presence. Lord Taylor's view is that this is a reasonable provision and gave an example. An officer arrests a man carrying away from a house hi-fi equipment belonging to the householder. The man declines to say why he has it. At trial his account is that the householder lent him the equipment for a party he was holding that evening. An innocent man questioned in those circumstances would surely have advanced the explanation straight away. If there is any good reason for not advancing it at the scene, the jury will have the opportunity to consider that reason before drawing an adverse inference.

Section 37 allows proper inferences to be drawn from the silence of a defendant who is arrested by a constable at a place and time reasonably suggesting that he is there because he has committed the offence under investigation. Lord Taylor uses the example of a girl raped at a student hostel. The police find the defendant in the hostel grounds. He gives no explanation for his presence on the premises. At trial he says that he had been working at the hostel. He had left his ladder at the back of the hostel and was returning to collect it for his next day's work elsewhere. Lord Taylor felt it was absurd for the jury to be told that his failure to mention that fact at the scene is something that they should not take into account. He feels that that is repugnant to common sense.

Lord Taylor was very strong in his support for the changes that are now contained in the Criminal Justice and Public Order Act 1994. He felt that they introduced common sense and realism that had been lacking up to the time of the changes.

In *R* v *Cowan* [1995] 3 WLR 818, Michael Mansfield QC argued before the Lord Chief Justice that s. 35 should only be used in exceptional circumstances when dealing with an accused who has exercised his right not to go into the witness box. This argument was not accepted.

Arguments in Favour of the Right to Silence being Retained

The right to silence is a safeguard for the vulnerable against wrongful convictions. The legal advice obtainable in the police station may not be a proper safeguard because it is either not available quickly enough or the standard of advice is not high enough.

Is the Right to Silence an Unnecessary Obstacle?

There is a feeling that an innocent person can have no excuse for not providing evidence of innocence at the earliest opportunity. It is the function of the police to investigate and the right to silence impedes their ability to investigate. These procedural rules in favour of the defendant make it harder to catch criminals, obtain the evidence and convict them. Silence alone will not convict a person because there must be a prima facie case. This was re-emphasised in *R* v *Cowan*.

Suspects can be safeguarded by tape recording and the availability of free legal advice in the police station.

Conclusion

Certainly academics such as Professor Murphy have criticised the effective abolition of the right to silence. There is no doubt that the abolition will lead to more persons being convicted. This is because after *R* v *Cowan* defendants will have to go into the witness box more often. Even educated persons who you would not expect to break down have broken down in the witness box. At the Australian trial of Lindy and Michael Chamberlain for killing their baby Azaria, Michael gave evidence. He was a religious preacher, experienced in public speaking and educated to degree level. After intense cross-examination he broke down and seemed to incriminate his wife. Both Chamberlains have always protested their innocence and their defence has always been that a dingo killed the baby. If that is true then this is an example of an innocent person breaking down in the witness box and being convicted. Those convictions devastated their lives.

QUESTION 2

'The presumption of innocence is an adequate safeguard of the rights of the accused despite recent changes to the law modifying the right to silence.' Discuss.

Commentary

The question requires a critical assessment of the criticisms of the removal of the right to silence and of the view that the presumption of innocence, that is, the prosecution bearing the burden of proof, is an adequate safeguard. The answer should distinguish between silence of the accused at the pre-trial and at the trial stage.

Suggested Answer

The phrase 'presumption of innocence' refers to the general rule in the House of Lords decision of *Woolmington* v *Director of Public Prosecutions* [1935] AC

462 that, subject to certain irrelevant exceptions, the prosecution bear the legal burden of proving all the elements of the offence. The 'right to silence' was referred to in *Rice* v *Connolly* [1966] 2 QB 414, where it was stated that there is no obligation on the accused to assist the police with their inquiries.

The right to silence of the accused may be regarded as an aspect of the privilege against self-incrimination. In the course of a criminal prosecution the right to silence can arise at two main stages: before the trial and at the trial. The common law position was originally enshrined in the Judges' Rules in 1912 and later in Code of Practice C by requiring a form of caution which ensured that before any interview where questions were put to a person suspected of a offence the right to silence was brought to the suspect's attention. In *Hall* v *R* [1971] 1 WLR 298, Lord Diplock stated that the caution merely serves to remind the accused of a right which he or she already possesses at common law. The Privy Council went on to state that a person is entitled to refrain from answering a question put to him for the purpose of discovering whether he has committed a criminal offence.

At common law the accused also has a right not to give evidence at his or her trial. By the Criminal Evidence Act 1898 the accused is also not compellable as a prosecution witness. This right is another aspect of the privilege against self-incrimination. However, the Criminal Justice and Public Order Act 1994 has brought about a change to the right to silence both at the pre-trial and the trial stage.

By s. 34 of the Act, when a suspect has been cautioned and questioned, if he relies on some fact in his defence which he could reasonably have mentioned at the time of questioning then an adverse inference that is appropriate in the circumstances can be drawn. Adverse inferences can also be drawn when a defendant has been charged and fails to mention facts which he later relies on his defence. Code of Practice C now sets out a new caution. Although it starts off by referring to the right of the suspect not to answer questions, it does caution the suspect that failure to mention facts can be detrimental to the defence at the later stage. The thinking of the government in introducing s. 34 is to prevent 'ambush defences'. This was also acknowledged judicially by Lord Lane CJ in *R* v *Alladice* (1988) 87 Cr App R 380, who said that the law since the Police and Criminal Evidence Act 1984 had gone too far in protecting the defendant particularly in respect of access to legal advice.

Section 36 of the 1994 Act deals with a suspect who has been lawfully arrested and found in possession of articles or with any substances or marks on his person, clothing or footwear. If the suspect is told in ordinary language of the constable's belief that the substance, object or mark is attributable to participation in an offence then appropriate inferences may be drawn from any failure or refusal to provide an answer.

Section 37 deals with the failure or refusal of the accused to account for his or her presence at a place at which the offence for which he or she was arrested was allegedly committed. The police must in ordinary language explain the effect of the section. The government took the view that experienced criminals abuse their rights and that it was only a matter of common sense that the inferences are drawn. It could be argued here that to a certain extent a burden is placed on the defendant to answer questions. The presumption of innocence is going to be quite inadequate here. However, s. 38(3) does provide that a conviction or a decision to transfer proceedings to the Crown Court for trial may not be based solely on an inference permitted by ss. 34, 35, 36 and 37. This offers some degree of protection in ensuring that there is some other evidence against the accused to sustain the charge.

It could be argued that these changes would pressure suspects leading to false confessions. The police would not be involved in neutral fact seeking but would be pressed to seek confessions.

Turning now to the position of the accused at trial, s. 35 of the 1994 Act provides that where the section applies the court or jury may regard the inference from failure to testify as in effect a further evidential factor in support of the prosecution's case. Section 35(4) does not render the accused compellable, and strictly the right to silence at trial still remains.

In *R* v *Cowan* [1995] 3 WLR 818, the Court of Appeal had to deal with two issues:

(a)   whether the discretion to draw inferences from silence under s. 35(3) should be open in the generality of cases or only exceptionally, and

(b)   if it was to apply in a jury trial what directions should be given by the judge.

In the course of the appeal counsel for some of the appellants had argued that s. 35 had the effect of reversing the burden of proof by imposing a burden on the defendant to give evidence at trial and in the circumstances the operation of the section should be reduced or marginalised as far as possible. The Court of Appeal did not accept the argument that the burden of proof was watered down. Instead it said that the prosecution had to establish a prima facie case before any question of the defendant testifying was raised. The court also made it clear that in summing up the judge must still follow *R* v *Bathurst* [1968] 2 QB 199 and make the following clear:

(a)   The burden of proof remained on the prosecution throughout to prove the offence beyond a reasonable doubt.

(b)   The defendant was entitled to remain silent, and that was his right and his choice.

(c)   Failure to give evidence was not on its own proof of guilt. This was presumed by s. 38(3) and (4).

(d)   After a prima facie case has been established, the jury can only come to an adverse inference if the defendant's silence could be attributed to the defendant having no answer or none that could stand up to cross-examination.

Conclusion

It may be said that although the presumption of innocence does still ensure that the prosecution bear the burden of proof, the defendant's position has indeed weakened. This is the case despite what the Court of Appeal stated in *R* v *Cowan*. The Court of Appeal left it as a matter of discretion for trial judges in the circumstances of individual cases to provide the appropriate directions on the inference to be drawn.

QUESTION 3

Manjit Singh was returning home one evening after a night out with his friends. As he walked along a street he heard some footsteps behind him and as he turned he was hit on the side of his face. The man who had hit him attempted to steal his wallet. Manjit struggled with him and hit the man's head against a wall. The man then ran away. Shortly afterwards a constable stopped Manjit and informed him that he was arresting him for assault.

(a)   You are asked to advise Manjit in custody on his rights in relation to answering police questions. Manjit has insisted on exercising his right to silence.

(b) A constable has suggested to Manjit that he has reason to believe that the steel bangles which Manjit had for religious reasons were for use as a weapon. Manjit refuses to answer such an insulting question. Advise Manjit.

Commentary

The question is framed as a problem and requires an account of the changes to the law in respect of the right to silence at the pre-trial stage.

Suggested Answer

(a) In dealing with the position of the suspect after 10 April 1995, Manjit must be advised that the right to silence has been modified. He should have been cautioned using the caution set out in para. 10.4 of Code of Practice C. This would have informed Manjit of his right to remain silent — 'You do not have to say anything' — but then he would have been informed that it may harm his defence if he does not mention when questioned something which he wants to rely on later in court.

In principle the right to remain silent is still provided for by the law, but the caution now sets out the effect of exercising that right, as provided by the Criminal Justice and Public Order Act 1994, s. 34. By this section, if an accused is cautioned and, on being questioned or on being charged with an offence, fails to mention any fact which is relied upon in the accused's defence which the accused could reasonably have been expected to mention at that stage then the appropriate inferences may be drawn.

If Manjit is going to rely on self-defence in respect of injuries caused to the other man then, even if he does not fully disclose his defence, he would be expected to mention the facts relating to the attack. These would obviously be facts that Manjit could reasonably be expected to mention during the questioning. The police would certainly mention the nature of the injuries sustained and also the circumstances surrounding the incident.

Manjit's interview will be tape recorded. There is a greater need for this now so as to ascertain the actual questions asked and to clarify what facts the accused did or did not mention.

Section 34 reverses the Court of Appeal decision of *R* v *Gilbert* (1977) 66 Cr App R 237. In this case the defendant when first interviewed by the police did not mention self-defence but he raised it as a defence at trial. The Court of

Appeal held it was an error to invite the jury by implication to draw an adverse inference against him for failing to mention the defence at an interview.

(b)   On the issue of Manjit's bangles, one is going to consider the provisions in s. 36 of the 1994 Act dealing with the failure of the accused to account for objects, substances or marks. Manjit must be warned that adverse inferences may be drawn from his refusal to answer questions about the bangles, provided the conditions set out in s. 36 are satisfied.

Section 36(1) applies if a person has been arrested by a constable, as Manjit has. It applies if the police inform the arrested person that the presence on his person of an object (the bangles) may be attributable to his participation in the commission of a specified offence (the assault). If the police then ask Manjit to account for the presence of the bangles, and explain in ordinary language the effect of failing or refusing to answer and he does refuse to answer then, under s. 36(2), adverse inferences may be drawn at trial.

It is difficult to predict what inferences it would be proper to draw from Manjit's refusal to account for the bangles. Much would depend on evidence of Manjit's reaction to the situation. The uncertainty makes it even more important for Manjit to answer the question but clearly it may not be possible to persuade him.

QUESTION 4

Plea bargaining and the use of sentence discounts to those who plead guilty are necessary if clogging up of the criminal courts is to be reduced. It is wrong to say that they stop defendants from having a fair trial. Discuss.

Commentary

This question expects students to be able to distinguish between plea bargaining and sentencing discounts. It has to be considered whether sentencing discounts are letting in plea bargaining by the back door. The Royal Commission's proposals for allowing a defendant to ask the judge what the maximum sentence would be if the defendant pleaded guilty were heavily criticised in some quarters for adding to the pressure to plead guilty.

Suggested Answer

If all defendants plead not guilty and exercise their right to a trial the court system will not be able to cope. Therefore there must be inducements to get people to plead guilty. A plea of guilty means that there is no trial and the convicted person proceeds straight to the sentencing stage.

The clogging up of the courts is detrimental to the quality of justice because it causes delays. Justice delayed is justice denied, especially where there are longer remands in custody for people awaiting trial. Delays affect the reliability of evidence and cause difficuties for victims who cannot begin recovery until after giving evidence.

Methods of reducing clogging up may also affect the quality of justice. The best solution would be to build enough courts and employ enough judges to hear the cases. However, no country has unlimited resources and therefore building more and more courts is not an adequate solution. Therefore other solutions within the system have to be considered. One such solution has been the use of plea bargaining and sentence discounts.

The question argues that these techiques are necessary, i.e., that this is the only way to reduce clogging up. Other ways, other than a massive court building programme could include encouraging or forcing more people to have their trials in the magistrates' courts. The problem with this idea is that the civil liberty groups do not believe that more offences should be tried summarily only but should at least be triable either way with the defendant having a right of election for Crown Court trial.

Plea Bargaining

Plea bargaining means that either the number of charges will be reduced if an accused pleads guilty, or the charges will be reduced to lesser charges, or a guilty plea will attract a sentence discount. Bargaining over the number of charges to be proceeded with or their nature would be between the prosecution and the defence lawyers.

The question argues that plea bargaining and sentence discounts are necessary.

Plea bargaining benefits the system and the guilty.

The system benefits because there has not been the time wasting and expense of a trial. Also there is the certainty of conviction.

But if the plea bargain and sentence discount have the effect of putting pressure on an innocent person to plead guilty then the system does have the effect of stopping defendants from having a fair trial.

Therefore it has to be considered whether there is any evidence of innocent persons being induced to plead guilty as a result of plea bargaining and sentencing discounts.

How Sentence Discounts Work in Practice

The case of *R* v *Cain* [1976] Crim LR 464 emphasises that a substantial discount can be obtained by those who admit guilt and cooperate fully with the police, for example, by providing information on accomplices or by asking for other offences to be taken into consideration. But the court did say that if an arrested person does not have much in the way of a defence to the charge then he or she cannot expect much by way of discount for pleading guilty. This case shows that the sentencing discount is not fixed. The value of the guilty plea to the courts gradually reduces as time goes by and the size of the discount reduces correspondingly. The full discount is only to be offered to those with something substantial in return. Where the evidence of guilt against the accused is very strong the court takes the approach that the defendant has no alternative but to plead guilty. But where the evidence is weaker then a greater reward would be more appropriate. In effect defendants who plead guilty where the evidence is weak have been induced to waive their right to put the prosecution to proof. It would seem that the weaker the prosecution case, the more likely it is that the defendant will put the prosecution to proof and the greater the sentencing discount that will be necessary so as to induce the defendant to plead guilty.

There is an argument that those pleading guilty are being rewarded for so doing, not that those pleading not guilty are being punished for contesting their case. However, the reality is that if you plead not guilty and are convicted then a longer sentence will be given compared to someone who pleaded guilty. Although the Court of Appeal has not been prepared to state specifically what the discount is, it would seem to be about one quarter to one third. Further the discount may have the effect of changing the nature of the sentence from custodial to non-custodial.

The case of *R* v *Turner* [1970] 2 QB 321 gives guidance on what is permitted concerning plea bargaining. Defence lawyers have to inform the defendant about the sentence discount. The advice would often include that a plea of guilty showing an element of remorse is a mitigating factor which may well enable the court to give a lesser sentence than would otherwise be the case. Lord Parker CJ in *R* v *Turner* did state that the defendant after having considered counsel's advice must have a complete freedom of choice as to whether to plead guilty or not guilty. The question that has to be considered is whether there is really such a freedom when there has been strong advice for counsel to plead guilty. Research by Baldwin and McConville (*Negotiated Justice* (1977)) has shown that a substantial proportion of defendants do change their plea to guilty because of persuasion from their defence lawyers. Therefore it can be argued that plea bargaining and sentence discounts do have the effect of undermining due process rights.

Role of the Trial Judge

If the judge gave a clear indication that would mean that defendants would clearly know where they stood. But the disadvantage would be that the impartiality of the judge would be brought into question by such communications. Further it might seem that the judge was trying to assist the prosecution in obtaining a conviction which would place even more pressure on the defendant to plead guilty. The law on plea bargaining and sentence discounts shows a compromise between due process and crime control values. A concern for due process seems to lie behind the prohibition on judges putting pressure on defendants directly. But the influence of the crime control model can be seen in the discount principle itself and in the leeway allowed to counsel in pressing the merits of pleading guilty on defendants directly.

In *R v Turner* the Court of Appeal held that a judge should not say precisely what sentence would follow a not guilty plea unless the sentence will be the same irrespective of how the defendant decides to plead. Negotiations between judges and counsel in which the judge indicates what reduction in sentence an accused might secure by pleading guilty are contrary to law. Research confirms that sentence bargaining frequently happens in the Crown Court. The Crown Court survey conducted for the Royal Commission on Criminal Justice showed that the majority of barristers and judges believed that there should be full and realistic discussion between counsel and the judges about plea and sentence. The person who most strongly affects the defendant's decision to plead guilty is the defendant's barrister whom the defendant might only see on the day of the trial. It has been argued that defence barristers arrive at court predisposed to settle the case for organisational reasons. Research suggests that some barristers convey a too pessimistic view of the likelihood of acquittal in order to increase pressure on defendants to plead guilty. In *R v Turner* the Court of Appeal said that barristers are supposed to tell their clients to plead guilty only if they accept that they are guilty. However, in practice, because of the pressure put on defendants the reality can be quite different.

Conclusion

If the pressure is such that innocent people feel obliged to plead guilty then the second part of the question is not correct in that the reality of the effect of plea bargaining and sentence discounts stops defendants from having a fair trial because there is no fair trial. Plea bargaining and sentence discounts may be factors reducing clogging up in the Crown Court but if they have the effect of innocent persons pleading guilty then that is too high a price to pay. The Royal Commission on Criminal Justice accepted that it would be naïve to suppose that innocent persons never pleaded guilty because of the prospect of the sentence discount.

QUESTION 5

Pleading guilty whilst maintaining innocence is a very unattractive feature of the English criminal justice system. We congratulate ourselves that we do not have the American method of plea bargaining because of its ills but nevertheless there are still innocent persons pleading guilty. Discuss.

Commentary

This question concerns an assessment of whether innocent people are pleading guilty in the English criminal justice system and there seems to be nothing that can be done about it.

Suggested Answer

England does not have full-blown plea bargaining in the American sense. In America the judge can become involved and indicate very precisely the type of sentence that he or she would impose should an accused plead guilty. Further the prosecution can suggest the appropriate sentence. The ill of this process is that innocent persons may be pressured to plead guilty.

In England there are sentence discounts for pleading guilty early. These are permitted by the Criminal Justice and Public Order Act 1994, s. 48.

The phrase 'plea bargaining' can have various meanings:

    (a)   The judge indicating sentence. There may be an agreement between the judge and the accused that if the accused pleads guilty to some or all of the offences charged then the sentence will or will not take a certain form. On the authority of *R* v *Turner* [1970] 2 QB 321 a guilty plea in such circumstances is a nullity and the conviction is liable to be quashed on appeal. So this type of plea bargaining is not permitted in England though it is in the USA. In England the judge can say what sentence he or she is minded to impose if the sentence will take the same form irrespective of how the defendant decides to plead. In *R v Turner*, Lord Parker CJ ruled that judges should never say they would impose a particular sentence on a plea of guilty and a more severe sentence on conviction following a plea of not guilty.

(b)   The prosecution indicating sentence. This could mean an undertaking by the prosecution that if the accused will admit to certain charges they will ask the judge to impose a lighter sentence and indicate the type of sentence. This form of plea bargaining is not possible under the English criminal justice system. The prosecution function is only to tell the judge the facts and not to suggest the appropriate sentence. This type of plea bargaining is available in the United States of America.

(c)   The prosecution accept a plea to a lesser offence. The plea bargain may refer to the prosecution agreeing with the defence that if the accused pleads guilty to a lesser offence they will accept the plea. This is acceptable in the English criminal justice system.

(d)   The prosecution not offering any evidence. This may refer to the prosecution agreeing not to proceed on one or more counts in the indictment if the accused will plead guilty to the remainder. This is allowed in the English criminal justice system.

Reasons for Sentence Discounts and Plea Bargaining

The reason for the English form of plea bargaining and sentence discounts is that if there is no incentive to plead guilty a defendant might as well take a chance with a trial so as to test whether the prosecution are able to secure a conviction. Therefore it is not usually in the public interest to spend time and money proving the accused guilty precisely as charged if the accused is prepared to admit the bulk of the case either by pleading guilty to a lesser offence or by pleading guilty to some counts but not all.

The advantages to the system are that the expense of a trial has been saved, and victims, witnesses and jury are spared the trauma of a trial. Further it means that those who do want to contest their cases can get to trial more quickly. Also it avoids the risk of the jury acquitting. These arguments make it necessary in the public interest that there be some form of inducement to plead guilty.

However, getting the right balance is fraught with difficulty because any system that encourages guilty persons to plead guilty will necessarily also induce weak-minded innocent people to plead guilty. It is not in the public interest that innocent persons should plead guilty. Research by Baldwin and McConville (*Negotiated Justice* (1977)) found that the advice of defence counsel is very important and that accused people changed their plea on advice received from counsel. Baldwin and McConville felt that in some of the cases the advice given had not been fair or proper. If counsel gives the impression that there is no hope or confidence, despite the accused's view that he or she is innocent this will put extra pressure on the accused.

Research was carried out for the Royal Commission on Criminal Justice, in which questionnaires were issued to judges, jurors, lawyers, police, court clerks and defendants in every contested case in the Crown Court during a period of two weeks in 1992. There were about 22,000 questionnaires relating to more than 3,000 cases. One of the things that the survey tried to find out was whether innocent people were pleading guilty. In cases where the defendant had pleaded guilty defence barristers were asked to consider whether they were dealing with an innocent defendant who had pleaded guilty so as to achieve a sentence discount or a reduction in the number of counts in the indictment. The results showed that some defence barristers (about 6 per cent) were concerned that they might have been dealing with such a case.

Defendants pleading guilty were also asked whether they had committed the offence which they had admitted. About 11 per cent said that they had not. The explanations that they gave in the questionnaire included being influenced by the sentence discount, an assurance from judge via the defence barrister that if there was a guilty plea there would be no prison sentence, wanting to get it over with, and pressure from defence lawyers. One of the reasons given is often one of the reasons why people confess in custody — wanting to get it over with.

The Crown Court survey confirms that the sentence discount continues to have a significant influence over defendants' decisions on plea irrespective of considerations of remorse. Guilty pleas can be got from unwilling defendants by sentence promises or threats.

Conclusion

Plea bargaining comes within the crime control model because it encourages the guilty to plead guilty and saves resources because it reduces the number of contested trials. Although lip-service is paid to the notion that the discount is based on an expression of remorse, the primary justification for the inducements to plead guilty is administrative expediency. A criminal justice system which places emphasis upon assumed innocence of the accused and the need for the prosecution to prove their case appears to be inconsistent with the existence of strong pressures to plead guilty.

13 Judicial Reasoning and Precedent

INTRODUCTION

In the English legal system, judges enjoy a higher status than their counterparts in the civil law systems of Europe, in part because of the more central role the judge plays in the development of precedent and the strict hierarchy of the courts where the opinions of more senior judges on appeal act as a subtle discipline on the more junior judges.

Both the vertical and horizontal nature of the doctrine of precedent must be appreciated. The vertical aspect of precedent is concerned with the way in which higher courts in the hierarchy bind courts lower down. The horizontal aspect is concerned with how certain courts such as the House of Lords and the Court of Appeal deal with their own earlier decisions.

The court structure is that the highest court for domestic law is the House of Lords. For European Community matters the highest court is the European Court of Justice whose decisions are binding on all United Kingdom courts. Decisions of the House of Lords are binding on all courts lower in the hierarchy. Decisions of the House of Lords can be departed from only by the House of Lords. Decisions of the Court of Appeal are generally binding on the Court of Appeal itself and binding on all courts lower in the hierarchy. The question of whether the Court of Appeal should be bound by its own decisions is the subject of the first question in this chapter. Decisions of individual High Court judges in the High Court are binding on the county courts but not on other High Court judges. However, they are of strong persuasive authority in the High Court and are usually followed. In the Crown Court the jury returns a verdict of guilty or not guilty. There is no precedent value in that. The function of the trial judge in the Crown Court is to make rulings on the law and these decisions are persuasive authority but are not binding. The decisions of the county courts and the magistrates' courts are not binding.

The part of the judgment that is binding is the *ratio decidendi* which is the legal principle necessary for the decision.

QUESTION 1

How far does precedent operate in the Court of Appeal? Should the court be free to adopt the same practice as the House of Lords in relation to its own previous decisions? Could the Court of Appeal issue a practice statement having a similar effect to that issued by the House of Lords in 1966? Would there be any point in doing so?

Suggested Answer

The Court of Appeal is an intermediate appellate court. The House of Lords is the highest appeal court. However, for practical purposes most appeals do not go further than the Court of Appeal. This is because appeals to the House of Lords are on points of law of public importance only and leave to appeal is necessary. Further there is the additional costs burden of taking the case to yet another appeal.

Doctrine of Precedent in the Court of Appeal

The Court of Appeal has to follow decisions of the House of Lords even if it thinks the House of Lords is wrong. This position is recognised by the Administration of Justice Act 1969, which provides a leapfrog procedure by which an appeal from the High Court can go direct to the House of Lords, if the High Court is bound by a Court of Appeal or House of Lords decision which it is arguable should no longer apply. For this procedure to apply, the trial judge must grant a certificate, all parties must agree and the House of Lords must give leave.

The Court of Appeal is generally bound by its own previous decisions. This is the position unless one of the exceptions in *Young* v *Bristol Aeroplane Co. Ltd* [1944] KB 718 applies. The exceptions are:

(a)   Where its own previous decisions conflict the Court of Appeal must decide which to follow and which to reject.

(b)   The Court of Appeal must refuse to follow a decision of its own which cannot stand with a decision of the House of Lords even though its decision has not been expressly overruled by the House of Lords.

(c)   The Court of Appeal need not follow a decision of its own if satisfied that it was given *per incuriam*, which means in ignorance or neglect of a relevant statutory provision or binding decision of the House of Lords or the Court of Appeal.

In 1966 the House of Lords issued *Practice Statement (Judicial Precedent)* [1966] 1 WLR 1234, which had the effect of freeing the House from the earlier rule laid down in *London Street Tramways Co. Ltd* v *London County Council* [1898] AC 375 that the House was bound by its own decisions. In the *London Street Tramways* case the House considered that it was in the public interest for there to be certainty in the law and a finality to litigation. From the 1930s onwards there was increasing judicial criticism of this practice and it had the disadvantage of making the law too rigid. Therefore in 1966 the practice was changed. The *Practice Statement* set out the reasons for the doctrine of precedent, namely, certainty in the law and the orderly development of legal rules. However, their lordships also recognised that a too rigid adherence to precedent may lead to injustice in a particular case. In future the House would normally treat its former decisions as binding but could depart from a previous decision when it appeared right to do so. Their lordships specifically stated that this was not intended to affect the use of precedent anywhere else other than the House of Lords.

In a press statement released at the same time was the *Practice Statement* more reasons for the change were set out. These were that the House of Lords could adapt to changing social conditions and pay more attention to decisions of superior courts in the Commonwealth. Further this change would bring the House of Lords in line with the practice of other superior courts in other countries including the USA.

This change in practice has been generally welcomed, but it was surprising that such an important change happened by a practice statement instead of by legislation. The House of Lords considered that it was only changing a self-imposed restraint by exercising its inherent jurisdiction as a court to change its own practice. Since 1966, the freedom of the House to depart from previous decisions has been used sparingly and only when clearly necessary.

Lord Denning MR, as head of the Court of Appeal (Civil Division), believed that the Court of Appeal should free itself from being bound by its previous decisions in the same way as the House of Lords had done. However, the House of Lords has clearly shown in later cases that it does not approve of the Court of Appeal being able to depart from its previous decisions or reviewing House of Lords' decisions.

Lord Denning tried to develop a principle that the Court of Appeal did not have to follow decisions of the House of Lords if it thought they were no longer good law (*Conway* v *Rimmer* [1967] 1 WLR 1031) or had, in the Court of Appeal's opinion, been decided *per incuriam* (*Broome* v *Cassell & Co. Ltd* [1971] 2 QB 354). Both approaches were expressly disapproved of by the House of Lords. In *Cassell & Co. Ltd* v *Broome* [1972] AC 1027 Lord Hailsham of St Marylebone LC stated in the strongest terms that he hoped that it would never be necessary again for the House of Lords to have to say that in the hierarchical system of courts each lower tier, including the Court of Appeal, must loyally accept the decisions of the higher tiers.

Lord Denning was further rebuked by the House of Lords in *Miliangos* v *George Frank (Textiles) Ltd* [1976] AC 443. The question in this case was whether to depart from the House of Lords' decision of *Re United Railways of Havana and Belga Warehouses Ltd* [1961] AC 1007, which had laid down that damages could only be awarded in sterling. The Court of Appeal in *Schorsch Meier GmbH* v *Hennin* [1975] QB 416 had not followed this decision and held that damages could be awarded in a foreign currency. The *Schorsch Meier* case did not go to the House of Lords but the same issue did in the *Miliangos* case. The House of Lords did then overrule the *United Railways* case but made it very clear that the Court of Appeal had been wrong to do so because only the House of Lords can review its own decisions.

Another technique of Lord Denning was to treat statements of the law in a House of Lords case as merely *obiter dicta* which are not binding because they are not part of the *ratio decidendi* of the case. The majority of the Court of Appeal in *Paal Wilson & Co. A/S* v *Partenreederei Hannah Blumenthal* [1983] 1 AC 854 took the approach that a passage by Lord Diplock in an earlier House of Lords case was an *obiter dictum* and therefore not binding. On appeal the House of Lords held that the relevant passage was *ratio* and therefore was binding. The Court of Appeal was reversed and the House of Lords refused to reconsider its earlier decision.

Lord Denning also argued that the Court of Appeal was no longer bound rigidly to follow its own previous decisions. In *Davis* v *Johnson* [1979] AC 264, Lord Denning justified this by arguing that if the Court of Appeal does not correct an error the House of Lords may never get an opportunity to do so. However, this argument failed in the House of Lords.

Scarman LJ in *Tiverton Estates Ltd* v *Wearwell Ltd* [1974] Ch 146 stated that allowing the Court of Appeal to depart from the previous decisions would lead to inconsistency and confusion. This is because the Court of Appeal sits in a number of divisions and if one refuses to follow another because it believes that other's decision is wrong there would be confusion and inconsistency. Therefore any error by the Court of Appeal should be corrected in the House of Lords. The benefit of this is that the House of Lords has the merit of being final and binding, subject only to its power to review its own decisions. 'The House of Lords, as the court of last resort, needs this power of review: it does not follow that an intermediate appellate court needs it' (per Scarman LJ in *Tiverton*).

Position of the Court of Appeal (Criminal Division)

In theory the doctrine of precedent works in the same way in both the civil and criminal divisions of the Court of Appeal. However, in practice, when a person's liberty is at stake the doctrine of precedent is not followed so rigidly in the criminal division. The approach taken is that the criminal division will not follow an earlier precedent if it is satisfied that the law was misapplied or misunderstood in it. This is the position even if the case is not within one of the exceptions laid down in *Young* v *Bristol Aeroplane Co. Ltd.*

Conclusion

In law there is nothing to stop the Court of Appeal adopting the same practice as the House of Lords. However since the retirement of Lord Denning his successors have not taken this approach and he himself was never able to persuade enough of his fellow judges that his views should become the accepted views. Lord Denning tried to use the House of Lords' practice statement as a justification for avoiding House of Lords decisions. He argued in *Conway* v *Rimmer* [1967] 1 WLR 1031 that the doctrine of precedent had been transformed by the practice statement. However, as an inferior court the Court of Appeal should still be bound by the House of Lords decisions and not be able to depart from them.

QUESTION 2

To what extent is it correct to say that the justification for the doctrine of precedent is that it guarantees that the law will remain certain and predictable?

Commentary

The question requires a consideration of the purpose of the doctrine of precedent and what it tries to achieve, and the balancing of conflicting objectives, namely, certainty on the one hand and the need to deal with changing social and economic conditions on the other hand.

Suggested Answer

Certainty and Predictability

The advantage of certainty is that it is possible to be more accurate in predicting what the law is in a particular area and therefore what the outcome would be if a matter was to be determined by the courts. Litigants can assess the nature and scope of their legal obligations and accurately predict the likely outcome of the dispute. Where the law is predictable parties can order their relationships based on this law and even avoid litigation because they know what its outcome will be.

Judges face a dilemma. The judge who applies an old rule to a new case may cause an injustice if that old rule is out of date. The rule might now be wrong or inappropriate or too harsh or completely irrelevant because of new circumstances. But if the judge simply does justice according to his or her own conscience then that would affect the fundamental principle that like cases should be treated alike. Further it would affect predictability and certainty which may lead to an increase in litigation clogging up the courts because more litigants would attempt to see if they could be successful.

There is an argument that predictability is essential to the rule of law, that everyone should be subject to the same law and know what the law is. This is achieved when there is certainty.

Too much unpredictability might also damage the reputation of the judiciary for impartiality in administering justice according to the law. This role is very important when dealing with legislation that is designed to give effect to policies which have been the subject of intense public and Parliamentary controversy, for example, industrial relations where there is plenty of room for differences of opinion about what is just and reasonable.

Precedent is a guide to the solution of new problems. However, it can be argued that precedent justice is unfair because it interferes with wiser conclusions of a later judge. Lord Denning was of the view that some rules developed in the nineteenth century, for example, in the law of contract, were now causing injustice and should be reformulated to take account of modern conditions. When Master of the Rolls, he tried to remove the limits of the doctrine of precedent in the Court of Appeal. He failed because the House of Lords did not approve of the approach and he could never convince enough of his fellow Court of Appeal judges to support his views on this. In his book *The Discipline of Law* (London: Butterworths, 1979) he stated that he was not against the doctrine of precedent but thought that a precedent should apply unless the judges thought it caused an injustice. However, that must introduce an element of uncertainty which will encourage wasteful litigation to test whether judges might agree that a precedent is unjust.

When the House of Lords was taking a rigid approach to the doctrine of precedent this was criticised and eventually the House had to change its position by issuing *Practice Statement (Judicial Precedent)* [1966] 1 WLR 1234. Rigidity could lead to injustice and restrict the development of the law. Therefore the courts have had to develop an approach that strikes a balance between certainty and rigidity. The House of Lords has tried to achieve this by saying that the *Practice Statement* would be sparingly used and being very firm that the Court of Appeal cannot take a similar approach.

The House of Lords has applied the *Practice Statement* when there has been a material change of circumstances, for example, departing from the principle in *Re United Railways of Havana and Regla Warehouses Ltd* [1961] AC 1007 that damages could only be awarded in sterling. In *Miliangos* v *George Frank (Textiles) Ltd* [1976] AC 443 the House of Lords held that damages can be awarded in a foreign currency. A new rule was needed because of changes in foreign exchange conditions, and especially the instability of sterling since 1961.

At first the House of Lords took the approach that it would not depart from an earlier decision merely because it was wrong and there was also concern about departing from an earlier decision if it had been decided fairly recently. However in *R* v *Shivpuri* [1987] AC 1 the House of Lords overruled within 12 months its own earlier decision in *Anderton* v *Ryan* [1985] AC 560. Lord Bridge who had sat in both appeals said:

> I am undeterred by the consideration that the decision in *Anderton* v *Ryan* was so recent. The *Practice Statement* is an effective abandonment of our pretention to infallibility. If a serious error embodied in a decision of this House has distorted the law, the sooner it is corrected the better.

In *Williams* v *Roffey Bros and Nicholls (Contractors) Ltd* [1991] 1 QB 1 the Court of Appeal had to deal with the case of *Stilk* v *Myrick* (1809) 2 Camp 317,

170 ER 1168. *Stilk* v *Myrick* was authority for the point that an existing contractual obligation could not be consideration for a later promise. *Williams* v *Roffey Bros and Nicholls (Contractors) Ltd* was a classic *Stilk* v *Myrick* situation. A main contractor had hired a subcontractor. The subcontractor had tendered for too low a price and was having difficulties completing the work. The main contractor agreed to pay the subcontractor more to complete the work. However, all the subcontractor was giving was his existing contractual obligation. The main contractor refused to pay arguing *Stilk* v *Myrick*. The Court of Appeal re-examined *Stilk* v *Myrick* and came to the view that the decision had really been influenced by policy factors at that time. The case had concerned the master of a ship who promised the crew that he would divide two deserters' wages amongst them if they worked the ship home safely. They did this but the master refused to pay the additional amount. The court took the approach that the crew were only giving what they were originally contractually obliged to do and that was not good consideration. However, the Court of Appeal took the approach that, provided the promisor received practical benefits for his promise and there was no duress then that could amount to consideration. Therefore the rule in *Stilk* v *Myrick* was modified so that it would now mean that the performance of an existing obligation would be good consideration for a promise provided the promisor obtained practical benefits and there was no duress.

Conclusion

The main reason for the doctrine of precedent is to promote certainty and predictability. However, these aims have to be reconciled with the need to do justice in individual cases and also to shape the law for the future. A balance has to be struck between these competing aims. The balance is the *Practice Statement* of 1966 and its practical operation by the House of Lords. Further there are other factors which the courts consider when deciding cases such as whether modern conditions would refine and limit the operation of an old rule, as happened in *Williams* v *Roffey Bros and Nicholls (Contractors) Ltd* [1991] 1 QB 1. It would really be the duty of legal advisers to advise whether the time has come to modify or discard an old common law rule. Then it has to be tested in the courts.

QUESTION 3

Precedent is a judicial fiction and as each case is different merely hides the operation of judicial discretion. Discuss.

Commentary

There is a view that the doctrine of precedent is something that can be circumvented when it becomes inconvenient. If it was that easy then the doctrine of precedent would be a fiction which it is not. It provides a structure although at times a flexible one.

Suggested Answer

The traditional view of an English judge, it is often said, is not to make law but to decide cases in accordance with existing legal rules. If it is indeed a function of the judge to decide cases in accordance with existing legal rules, is this a matter of practice, that is, of custom, or a matter of law?

It must be stated at the outset that the answer to this question cannot be definite. Many writers, and especially Lord Lloyd in his work *Lloyd's Introduction to Jurisprudence* (Sweet and Maxwell), take the stand that the rules of precedent are merely rules of practice. Although precedent may be defined as the binding nature of decisions it is not correct to state merely that 'decisions' are binding. The *ratio decidendi* may be defined as the statement of law that is applied to the legal problems raised by the facts as found, upon which the decision is based. Judicial discretion plays an important part in ascertaining the *ratio decidendi* as first the judge must infer the material facts of a case and from them make necessary inferences. Then the principles of law have to be considered. It is the combined operation of the two elements (facts and law) that produce the *ratio decidendi*. A court can always avoid the binding nature of precedent by distinguishing the facts of the case before it from that of a previous case. An illustration of this approach can be found in the Divisional Court decision of *England* v *Cowley* (1873) 2 LR 8 Ex 126 and the Court of Appeal case of *Oakley* v *Lyster* [1931] 1 KB 148. In *England* v *Cowley* it was held that although the defendant did not allow the plaintiff to remove goods from the defendant's premises, this was not conversion as there was no absolute denial of the plaintiff's title. The Court of Appeal in *Oakley* v *Lyster* distiguished *England* v *Cowley* by holding that there was a conversion when the defendant refused to allow the plaintiff to remove material from the defendant's land because the defendant asserted his own title to the material, which was equivalent to denying the plaintiff's title. The distinguishing of a case can, therefore, at times, be very fine. The process of distiguishing could be said to be a factor that enables the doctrine of precedent to remain flexible and adaptable. It can be argued that distinguishing emphasises the judicial discretion that lies at the root of the doctrine of precedent. Each case, as suggested by the present question, is different, but in exceptional cases when the facts of two cases are indistiguishable courts describe them as being 'on all fours'. But again it can be argued that it is judicial discretion that enables a judge to decide if a case is 'on all fours'.

With regard to appellate court decisions, when more than one judgment is delivered, each member of the court, for example, the Court of Appeal, could arrive at the same conclusion yet give different reasons. The practice is for the judgment of the majority to be adopted and it is this judgment that provides the *ratio*. But the position is complicated when no one reason is favoured by the majority. If a statement of law in a decision is not necessary for the decision then a subsequent court is not obliged to follow it. The statement of law would be treated as an *obiter dictum*. A principle of law may also be *obiter* if, for instance, the principle was stated on facts which are not found to exist in the particular case. A court may also state a principle of law too widely. In such a case the principle would only apply to the extent of the facts of the case. In *Hillyer* v *St Bartholomew's Hospital* [1909] 2 KB 820, the Court of Appeal held a hospital was not liable for the negligence of a consultant surgeon. The reason was that the hospital could not control the way in which he performed his work. In *Hillyer* v *St Bartholomew's Hospital* this principle was stated broadly and was stated to cover any doctor in the hospital's employ. However, in a subsequent case the Court of Appeal limited the principle only to consultant surgeons and not to resident surgeons whose work can be controlled by the hospital as employer (*Cassidy* v *Ministry of Health* [1951] 2 KB 343). The principle stated in *Hillyer* v *St Bartholomew's Hospital* was broader than was necessary for the decision. From the above discussion it is apparent that the concept of precedent does depend on judicial discretion. However, to treat precedent as nothing more than a judicial fiction would not be accurate as a system of precedent is required in order to achieve legal certainty. The principle of *ratio decidendi* and the hierarchy of the courts are well defined to achieve this legal certainty. Lord Diplock in the House of Lords case of *Davis* v *Johnson* [1977] AC 264 emphasised that the doctrine of *stare decisis* or precedent has to hold the field. Existence of judicial discretion on the other hand can be supported on the basis that it is necessary if the system of precedent is to retain a certain amount of flexibility.

Conclusion

When one considers the doctrine of precedent one realises that judicial discretion is involved and would seem to be operating like a fiction. However, the judges are working within a structure and subject to principles, namely, the principles or rules of the doctrine of precedent. The judge will consider the authorities that counsel argue are binding in the instant case and the judge arrives at what he or she considers to be the correct application of the law to the fact situation. This works well in areas where the judges consider the law is just and they are happy to apply earlier precedents. However, in situations where they feel that the law is not just then the judges attempt to bypass the authority in that area.

QUESTION 4

Twenty five years ago the House of Lords enunciated a legal principle which was the indisputable *ratio* of the decision in question. The principle has since been applied both by the Court of Appeal and at first instance. Last year, however, the Court of Appeal disregarded all these previous decisions and refused to apply the principle. No appeal against the decision was made to the House of Lords. The same issue has now arisen in a new case.

Discuss how the rules of precedent should be applied: (a) at first instance, (b) in the Court of Appeal, and (c) in the House of Lords.

Commentary

This is an interesting question which requires an analysis of what happens when there are conflicting decisions and how each court would deal with a conflicting decision.

Suggested Answer

(a) At First Instance

The doctrine of precedent requires that a lower court in the hierarchy of courts is bound by the previous decisions of a higher court. On the facts of this question the judge at first instance must deal with the following problems:

(a) there is a House of Lords case that has been decided differently from the Court of Appeal decision, and

(b) there are two conflicting Court of Appeal decisions.

Taking the first problem in isolation, according to Lord Simon of Glaisdale in *Miliangos* v *George Frank (Textiles) Ltd* [1976] AC 443, the judge at first instance must follow the decision of the immediately higher court. The reasoning is that the judge cannot declare that a decision of the Court of Appeal is wrong and must assume that it resolved any apparent conflict with the House of Lords decision.

The judge would then have the difficulty of deciding which of the two conflicting Court of Appeal decisions should be followed. The judge could proceed on the basis that there is House of Lords authority for the legal principle and therefore follow the House of Lords decision as this is the highest authority. But in order to adopt this reasoning the judge would have to hold that the Court of Appeal's latest decision was made in ignorance of the House of Lords decision. It can be argued that the proper course for the judge to take is to apply the most recent Court of Appeal decision even if it conflicts with the House of Lords authority. The Court of Appeal can resolve the question on appeal.

Another option that might be available, would be for the judge to distinguish the instant case from one of the Court of Appeal decisions so as to prevent any conflict with the other. However, this may not be possible.

(b)   In the Court of Appeal

The Court of Appeal is bound by the decisions of the House of Lords. However, the main issue here would be whether the Court of Appeal can overrule its own previous decisions. In *Young* v *Bristol Aeroplane Co. Ltd* [1944] KB 718 Lord Greene MR cited three exceptions where the Court of Appeal would not be bound by its own previous decision. These are:

(i)   Where there are two conflicting decisions, the court may choose which to follow. The decision not being followed would be deemed to be overruled.

(ii)   The Court of Appeal is bound to refuse to follow its own decisions which though not expressly overruled cannot stand with a later House of Lords decision.

(iii)   The Court of Appeal is not bound to follow any of its decisions which were given *per incuriam*.

On the facts of this question it would appear that the more recent judgment of the Court of Appeal is clearly inconsistent with the House of Lords decision made some 25 years ago. As such the second exception identified by Lord

Greene would not arise. It is, however, submitted that the position here is not clear as Lord Greene in setting out the principles had not considered the situation where the inconsistent House of Lords decision is not a subsequent one. It is submitted that the single maverick decision of the Court of Appeal which is inconsistent with a House of Lords decision on a legal principle that has stood for about 25 years should not be allowed to stand. Thus the Court of Appeal should follow the House of Lords judgment. Since the point is not settled the Court of Appeal may also take the opportunity to rely on the first of Lord Greene's exceptions to decide on which of its conflicting decisions it wishes to follow. It is important to note that the House of Lords in the decision of *Davis* v *Johnson* [1979] AC 264 unequivocally and unanimously approved the principles in *Young* v *Bristol Aeroplane Co. Ltd.*

(c) In the House of Lords

Since the *Practice Statement (Judicial Precedent)* [1966] 1 WLR 1234 the House of Lords has been free to depart from its previous decisions whenever it appears right to do so. The House of Lords, it can be argued, has always been very cautious in using this *Practice Statement.* In *Jones* v *Secretary of State for Social Services* [1972] AC 944, it was explained by Lord Simon of Glaisdale that it was a power that is to be exercised 'most sparingly'. However, the House has also stated that where there is a serious error, the sooner it is corrected the better (*R* v *Shivpuri* [1987] AC 1).

The House of Lords could also avoid being bound by its previous decision by distinguishing the instant case, if that is possible. Also it could reject its previous decision if it was given *per incuriam*. Alternatively, the House of Lords may reaffirm that the legal principle enunciated 25 years ago is the correct position and overrule the Court of Appeal decision that refused to apply the principle.

14 Law Reform, Legislation and Statutory Interpretation

INTRODUCTION

Proposals for new legislation may be made by the Law Commission or a Royal Commission, from a pressure group or a civil liberty group, from political pressures such as the Conservative government wanting to maintain its position as the party of law and order which has been the driving force behind many of the changes concerning criminal justice.

This chapter will first consider law reform and how proposals become law. Once a statute becomes law then it is the function of the judges to enforce and interpret that law. Not all statutes are crystal clear. If a provision in a statute is ambiguous, the judge must interpret it before applying it. This is known as judicial reasoning or statutory interpretation.

The impact of the European Union on statutory interpretation also needs to be considered. The UK joined the European Community with effect from 1 January 1973. The UK acceded to the Treaty of Rome (known as the EC Treaty) and the UK's treaty obligations were enacted into UK law by the European Communities Act 1972. The treaty obligations apply directly in the UK because of s. 2(1) of the European Communities Act 1972. There are two main types of EC law, namely, Regulations and Directives. Regulations apply directly in the UK by virtue of s. 2(1) and deal with matters such as fishing quotas. Directives deal with more substantial changes in the law. The EC allows member States to implement Directives through national legislation and the member State can decide how to provide for the enforcement of remedies. For example, the rights created by Directives on sex discrimination are enforceable in Britain through industrial tribunals.

By s. 2(2) of the European Communities Act 1972, European community obligations such as Directives can be implemented as part of UK law by delegated legislation.

By s. 3 of the European Communities Act 1972, European law will be treated as law to be applied by the UK courts. As the highest court for the enforcement of the European Community treaty obligations and law is the European Court of Justice, English courts have to apply the decisions of this court when they are dealing with the interpretation of European Community law. As a result of this, British judges have been exposed to and have applied such principles as the primacy of European Community law over UK law and also European methods of statutory interpretation such as the purposive approach. This exposure must eventually spill over at times as to how they approach purely domestic law which has not yet been affected by European Community law.

QUESTION 1

Describe the processes by which proposals for legislation emerge and become law. To what extent do the main law reform organisations play in this process and to what extent is this satisfactory?

Commentary

Law reform and developments in the law are topics that are inherent in the English legal system syllabus. Even if it is not tested as a topic on its own in a specific question, it is still an area that you have to know generally as part of your study of the English legal system. When considering law reform and developments in the law one can take case studies from other areas of the syllabus such as miscarriage of justice.

Suggested Answer

There are various ways that proposals for legislation can emerge and become law. Legislation is the product of Parliament and what has to be considered is the sources or forces that lead to any particular piece of reforming legislation being introduced into Parliament and being passed by Parliament. These would include the party political agenda of the government and pressures on governments from, for example, pressure groups and the work of official bodies such as government-appointed committees, Law Commission reports and reports by royal commissions.

Legislation that may be described as party political agenda law is that which is contained in a manifesto on which a party won a general election. It would include law that is part of the ideology of the party. Examples of such law would be legislation by the Conservative government in the 1980s reducing trade union powers which would be described as reforming trade union powers, and legislation altering the organisation of education. Another clear example of this is legislation concerning privatisation.

Party political agenda law can be compared with lawyers' law which covers laws and proposals for law reform that are not hot party political issues.

There is an overlap between the two in some areas, for example, the friction between criminal justice procedures that are thought to be too liberal and might lead to too many acquittals and changes that might win votes such as effectively limiting the right of silence and being seen to be tough on crime. This is a suitable area for a Royal Commission which is normally set up to allow for a far more in-depth consideration in a sensitive area where different parties have widely different views about reform and hopefully produce a report that is an acceptable compromise.

The Law Commission generally deals with lawyers' law and so does not generally generate political heat.

Some legislation which is political agenda law will go straight to the Bill stage and be introduced in Parliament by the Minister responsible for the Bill's passage through Parliament. Generally it will be mentioned in the Queen's speech at the opening of the Parliamentary year that this Bill is going to be introduced in the forthcoming Parliamentary session.

For proposals that are more controversial or on which the government wants views, a Green Paper may be issued. This is for the purpose of obtaining feedback, discussion and consultation on government proposals. After this a White Paper will be published. This is where the government's proposals are firmer and the reasons and justifications for the changes are set out. There is no obligation on the government to do this: the government can go straight to the issuing of a White Paper or go straight to the Bill stage. It will really depend on how government wants to approach a particular matter.

Once a Bill has been introduced into Parliament, it will have three readings in the House of Commons and the Bill will have to pass these stages. The first reading is formal and there is no debate. The second reading involves a general debate on the policy of the whole Bill. This debate is by the whole House. A Bill normally goes through a committee stage which would generally be a clause-by-clause examination of the Bill in standing committee. Amendments can be proposed at this stage. Then there is a report stage where amendments made in committee are reported, then confirmed or reversed. Then there is the third reading where there is brief debate on the amended Bill. The Bill will then go to the House of Lords. It is possible for a Bill to start in the House of Lords. But most Bills start in the House of Commons. In the House of Lords there is the same procedure. If the House of Lords makes amendments then the Bill has to go back to the House of Commons for a consideration of the Lords' amendments. If they are accepted then the Bill then goes for the Royal Assent and becomes an Act of Parliament. If the Lords' amendments are rejected by the House of Commons then usually the Lords give way and the Bill then proceeds to Royal Assent.

Law Reform Bodies

The law reform bodies can be divided into governmental and non-governmental. Of the government-appointed or created bodies there are permanent law reform bodies and ad hoc bodies.

The main non-governmental bodies include Justice and Liberty which produce reports on various matters. For example, Justice has produced reports on the need for an independent prosecution service, changes needed in judicial appointments and the need for a criminal cases review commission. Liberty has produced reports concerning the need for a Bill of Rights and reform of the judiciary.

Justice's ideas have not been accepted directly but have had an indirect impact. For example, its representations to the Royal Commission on Criminal Procedure concerning the need for an independent prosecution service were accepted by the Royal Commission. These were contained in the Royal Commission's report which was accepted by the government, and the Prosecution of Offences Act 1985 was passed leading to the creation of a nationwide independent prosecution service.

Ad hoc bodies are set up for a specific purpose and then disbanded once they have reported. The Committee on the Distribution of Criminal Business between the Crown Court and the Magistrates' Courts was set up in the 1970s to deal with the problem of the Crown Court not being able to cope with its workload. The Committee made recommendations many of which were accepted and these became law in the Criminal Law Act 1977. In the 1980s the Fraud Trials Committee was set up chaired by Lord Roskill. This committee made a series of recommendations, including the creation of a fraud trials tribunal instead of trial by judge and jury, the creation of a Serious Fraud Office for better prosecution of these cases, and that small theft should become a summary only offence. Of these recommendations only the creation of the Serious Fraud Office was accepted and implemented by the Criminal Justice Act 1987. The Civil Justice Review in the 1980s made recommendations which were enacted in the Courts and Legal Services Act 1990. The Efficiency Scrutiny Committee made recommendations which formed the basis of the Legal Aid Act 1988.

A royal commission is an important ad hoc committee in the sense that it is the most prestigious and will have greater publicity generally. It will also have more resources.

The Royal Commission on Legal Services from 1976 to 1979 considered the practices of the legal profession. It recommended that the legal profession should keep its existing practices such as the solicitors' conveyancing monopoly and the Bar's exclusive rights of audience in the higher courts. Eventually the government did the opposite to these recommendations.

With regard to the criminal justice system there was the Royal Commission on Criminal Procedure from 1978 to 1981. Its recommendations were in principle accepted but there were changes concerning the way some of those recommenations were actually implemented in the Police and Criminal Evidence Act 1984. The Royal Commission on Criminal Justice was set up in 1991 and reported in 1993. Both commissions had been set up as a result of highly publicised miscarriages of justice. Both had recommended that the right to silence should not be limited on the grounds that it would put vulnerable suspects at risk. However, the Conservative government wanted to show that it had a strong law and order policy, being tough on crime, and accepted the view of the police that experienced criminals could exploit the system by remaining silent. So the right to silence was ended by the Criminal Justice and Public Order Act 1994. Other recommendations that have not yet been accepted by the government include, that s. 8 of the Contempt of Court Act 1981 should be amended to allow for legitimate research into the jury, that there should be racially balanced juries in certain circumstances, and that the accused should no longer have a right to elect trial by jury when charged with a triable either way offence. The recommendation that defendants should lose the right to elect trial by jury generated much opposition from civil liberty groups.

The recommendations of these royal commissions were presented on the basis of a package that would ensure the right balance in the criminal justice system between the need to convict guilty persons and the need to acquit innocent persons. When the government does not accept all of the recommendations and picks and chooses then one of the benefits of the Royal Commission goes, namely, to try to present a better overall solution in a particular area.

There are certain deficiencies concerning royal commissions. They are limited by their terms of reference. They may be too slow because it will be many years from the date of setting up to the date when legislation is finally passed. They must try to reach a compromise which does not satisfy everyone. It was for these reasons that no royal commission was set up during Mrs Thatcher's time as Prime Minister.

The main permanent law reform body is the Law Commission. This was set up by the Law Commission Act 1965. The aim was to improve the arrangements concerning the consideration of law reform by charging the body with the duty of keeping the law as a whole under review and making recommendations for its systematic reform. Its prime duty is to consider law reform. Its creation was a response to pressure from lawyers who had published a book in 1963 called *Law Reform Now*, edited by Gerald Gardiner and Andrew Martin, which drew attention to many inadequacies and injustices in the then state of the law.

The Law Commission is independent with full-time members. It prepares reports on particular areas and issues consultation papers. The final report generally contains a draft Bill. A lot of its major work has not been enacted, for example, the draft criminal code. It was the aim of the Law Commission to prepare codes but the Commission is now taking a piecemeal approach. Some work has been enacted such as the Unfair Contract Terms Act 1977 and the Criminal Attempts Act 1981. There has been some improvement in the Parliamentary procedures to get some of its Bills enacted. These Bills are generally considered to be not politically controversial. It can be agreed that they are suitable for referral to the Commons second reading committee and the Lords special standing committee and in those circumstances a bill is less likely to fail for want of time. For example, the Law Commission Bill which became the Law of Property (Miscellaneous Provisions) Act 1994 was passed in this manner. It took over an hour on the floor of the House of Lords, a few minutes in the House of Commons and just over seven hours in the House of Lords special standing committee.

In the 1994/5 Parliamentary session five Bills based on Law Commission reports were introduced. They were the Private International Law (Miscellaneous Provisions) Bill (dealing with polygamy in cases with foreign interests, payment of debts in foreign currency), the Family Homes and Domestic Violence Bill (civil remedies for domestic violence), the Civil Evidence Bill (permitting hearsay evidence in civil courts), the Wills (Effect of Divorce) Bill (divorced spouses and their former partners' wills), and the Distribution of Estates Bill (rules of intestacy). One of those Bills has fallen and ironically has transgressed on sensitive political territory, namely, the Bill concerning domestic violence. This was because it would have put cohabitees on the same basis as married couples and it was thought by some politicians that this would further undermine the family.

Conclusion

There are many law reform bodies. Their role is purely to advise and recommend. The government will then decide its reaction to those proposals and to what extent those recommendations fit into their political agenda and objectives. The Royal Commission on Criminal Justice would have been aware of that agenda and tried to produce a package of reforms that could fit in with it at least to some extent. Despite that the goverment has ignored some of its key views and has done the opposite of some its recommendations, for example, concerning the right to silence.

QUESTION 2

How important and significant to law making are the following: (a) the United Kingdom's membership of the European Community, (b) legislation, (c) delegated legislation, and (d) case law?

Commentary

This question requires a consideration of all the ways that laws are made in the UK together with an assessment of which is the most significant today. There must be an examination of Parliamentary and delegated legislation and the relationship between Parliament and the judiciary, especially in the light of the United Kingdom's membership of the European Community.

Suggested Answer

Legislation

Legislation is one of the principal sources of law. A constitutional law principle has developed of Parliamentary sovereignty or supremacy which means that the highest law-making body is Parliament and there is no higher body. This was settled by the Bill of Rights 1688 (*British Railways Board* v *Pickin* [1974] AC 765, HL). Because of this constitutional position, the judges cannot strike down legislation, they can only interpret it and enforce it. This is certainly the position with regard to purely domestic legislation. It is, however, not the position with regard to European Community treaty obligations, to European Community law that applies directly in the United Kingdom, or has been enacted into United Kingdom law, or to the law that has been developed by the European Court of Justice which is the highest court for the interpretation of the EC Treaty and EC law. This has been the position since the enactment of the European Communities Act 1972.

EC law has to be treated as the highest form of law so as to give effect to the aims of the EC which is that certain EC laws are to be the same throughout the community. The European Community has its own law-making powers, its own executive and its own court. The European Court of Justice in the case of *Van Gend en Loos* v *Nederlands Belastingadministratie* (case 26/62) [1963] ECR 1 stated that 'the Community constitutes a new legal order, the States have limited their sovereign rights, albeit within limited fields'. The effect of this has been that courts have had to suspend the operation of a British Act of Parliament that might conflict with European Community law (*R* v *Secretary of State for Transport, ex parte Factortame Ltd (No. 2)* (case C–213/89) [1991] 1 AC 603). Under national law the British courts had no such power. There is a procedure known as an art. 177 reference which can be made by a British court to the European Court of Justice on any question about EC law. Such a reference was made in the *Factortame* case. The European Court of Justice held that under EC law a national law (whether legislative, judicial or administrative in character) must be set aside by a national court if it prevents the application of EC law.

In *R* v *Secretary of State for Employment, ex parte Equal Opportunities Commission* [1995] 1 AC 1, a declaration was sought that the United Kingdom was in breach of Community law obligations in relation to art. 119 of the EC Treaty and the Equal Pay and Equal Treatment Directives. The alleged breach concerned the Employment Protection (Consolidation) Act 1978 which discriminated between full-time and part-time employees in relation to redundancy pay and compensation for unfair dismissal. The House of Lords ruled that English law was incompatible with Community law, but declined to hold that the Secretary of State was in breach of Community law or to strike down the Act.

Thus where EC law applies it is going to displace UK law and the courts will have no choice but to uphold that position. However, the fields where EC law currently applies are very limited, having been mainly confined to employment law, company law, discrimination law concerning men and women in the workplace, and environmental law. Recently in contract law there has been the EC Directive on Unfair Terms in Consumer Contracts. Thus still at the moment the main source of law is legislation passed by the UK Parliament (primary legislation) and delegated legislation made by some person or body other than Parliament.

Private Members' Bills

Private Members' Bills concern a matter that an individual member of Parliament believes to be important. They can be introduced into Parliament by a member of either the House of Commons or the House of Lords, for example, in the 1994/95 Parliamentary session Lord Lester of Herne Hill QC introduced a Bill to enact the European Convention on Human Rights into UK law as a Bill of Rights.

MPs take part in a ballot at the start of a new session of Parliament and only those who are successful may introduce a private member's Bill. Those that are not successful may use the '10-minute rule' under Standing Order 19 of the House, which permits a member to put down a motion at the start of public business on certain days for leave to introduce a Bill. However, such Bills rarely become law.

In terms of their significance as a source of law private members' Bills are insignificant. However, some very controversial matters have been introduced as private members' Bills, for example, the Abortion Act 1967, which would be too sensitive to become part of a main party political agenda. Introducing a private member's Bill may publicise the issues involved, and even though the proposal may not become law, it might eventually put the issue on the political agenda so that eventually the issues will be addressed in later legislation.

Delegated Legislation

The power to create delegated legislation comes from an Act of Parliament, which gives power to others, such as a government Minister or local authority to make law by way of delegated legislation. Delegated legislation made by a Minister will take the form of rules, regulations or orders. These are made as statutory instruments. Local authorities make by-laws. A validly enacted piece of delegated legislation has the same legal force and effect as the Act of Parliament under which it is enacted but it only has effect to the extent that the enabling Act authorises it.

Delegated legislation has increased in importance and significance since the nineteenth century because Parliament has neither the time nor the expertise to legislate in detail in all areas. The parent Act would be concerned with general principles but leave certain details to be worked out by the relevant Minister. For example, by s. 11 of the Courts and Legal Services Act 1990 the Lord Chancellor is given the power to introduce by order rights of audience or the right to conduct litigation by lay persons with regard to certain types of proceedings in the county court. The Lord Chancellor exercised this power cautiously by introducing the Lay Representatives (Rights of Audience) Order 1992 which allowed lay persons rights of audience in small claims proceedings.

The Lord Chancellor took a cautious approach and will be monitoring the success of this before exercising his powers further.

Parliament can still exercise some control over delegated legislation if the parent Act lays down that before a statutory instrument can come into force it has to be laid before both Houses of Parliament and passed by a vote of each House. The only weakness of this process is that Parliament cannot amend parts of the statutory instrument, it can only reject in total or pass in total. Also votes on statutory instruments are dealt with towards the end of the Parliamentary sitting day when there are not many members in attendance.

Most statutory instruments do not need to go through this type of process but are simply laid before Parliament and automatically become law after a period of 40 days unless a resolution to annul them is passed.

Delegated legislation has the advantages of speed, lower cost and use of the delegate's expertise in formulating detail leaving Parliament to address itself to policy and general principles.

Case Law

The judges do not enjoy the same freedom to make new law as is possessed by Parliament. Parliament is the supreme lawmaker for domestic law and the courts play a subordinate role. However, the courts too have a role to play in developing the law. The courts are limited by the facts of the cases before them and so can only develop the law on a piecemeal basis. The courts are generally reluctant to extend the boundaries of the common law beyond established precedent. This approach promotes certainty but has the disadvantage that the courts may fail to take account of changing needs and attitudes. Further, policy is said to be the province of Parliament. Therefore it will be for Parliament to promote major changes in the law. In recent years there has been a reluctance on the part of the courts to deal with long-established rules of the common law on the basis that Parliament is the appropriate place for such matters. For example, in *C (A Minor) v Director of Public Prosecutions* [1996] 1 AC 1, the House of Lords had to consider whether to abolish the additional burden on the prosecution to prove 'mischievous discretion' in addition to the *mens rea* and *actus reus* of a criminal offence. The House of Lords considered that any change in the law was a matter within the exclusive remit of Parliament. Another case, *R v Clegg* [1995] 1 AC 482, concerned an army private who was raising self-defence to a charge of murder. He had been on checkpoint duty in Northern Ireland and a car was about the break through the checkpoint. He and others opened fire. He was still firing after the car went past. On the evidence it was found that the fatal shot was fired after the car had gone past, when he was no longer in danger and so he could not rely on self-defence. He had also used excessive force. The House of Lords considered whether it should declare that a person who killed in self-defence but with excessive force should be able to have a charge of murder reduced to manslaughter. The House of Lords was not prepared to do this, taking the approach that the law is settled and that any change was a matter for Parliament to consider, especially as the question is part of the wider issue whether the mandatory life sentence for murder should be maintained.

In some cases there is evidence that the courts are prepared to change a common law rule, for example, the House of Lords recognised the possibility of the crime of rape within marriage (*R* v *R* [1992] 1 AC 599). This was a departure from the common law which contained an irrebuttable presumption that the wife had consented to all acts of intercourse on marriage.

There is an argument that as the judges created the common law they can be left to reform it. However, as seen above, there is still some reluctance with long-standing common law rules. The judges cannot reform statutory provisions. They can only express their dissatisfaction with their operation, for example, how the mandatory life sentence for murder has been harsh on some such as Private Clegg.

The judges interpret the meaning to be placed on statutory provisions when a case comes to court. Provisions can be interpreted narrowly or widely and this gives a judge potentially great power in determining the future scope of the law. When judges do this they add to the body of case law which may assist future courts in deciding disputes.

Conclusion

Whilst it may be arguable that certain types of legislation are more important than others it can be clearly seen that each method has its role and utility. In reality all these types of legislation are important and have their significance in contributing to the development of the law and law reform.

QUESTION 3

What principles are employed when statutes are interpreted by the courts? Is one principle paramount?

Commentary

This question requires a discussion of the various principles of interpretation with a conclusion as to whether there are any discernible dominant principles. It has to be realised that statutory interpretation is not a precise art but it involves the application of certain rules.

Suggested Answer

When involved in the interpretation of statutes, the courts employ various principles. Although these are often referred to as 'rules' of interpretation they are ultimately nothing more than guiding principles.

It has been observed by Sir Carleton Allen in his book *Law in the Making*, 7th ed. (Oxford: Clarendon Press, 1964) that '... we are driven, in the end, to the unsatisfying conclusion that the whole matter ultimately turns on impalpable and indefinable elements of judicial spirit or attitude'.

Main Approaches to Statutory Interpretation

The judicial spirit or attitude in approaching the question of interpretation has often been categorised into three main approaches: the literal rule, the golden rule, and the mischief rule. The European purposive approach has not yet been fully accepted by the English courts.

Literal Rule

This is the traditional method of statutory interpretation in the English legal system except for cases involving European Community law. This rule of interpretation is the starting point and in that sense can be argued to be the dominant approach in the English system. The literal rule requires a statute to be interpreted literally, that is, the words of a statute are to be given their ordinary and natural meaning.

Whilst it is the function of Parliament to legislate it is the function of the courts to interpret legislation and the courts have to construe a statute in accordance with the words used by the legislature no matter what the outcome of such an interpretation would be. This means that the judge starts with the literal or grammatical meaning of the words in the statute. The literal rule provides by and large a reasonable interpretation of a statute. However, if a statute is carelessly drafted then the rule can produce manifest absurdity.

In *Inland Revenue Commissioners* v *Hinchy* [1960] AC 748, Lord Reid insisted that the courts must apply the words of Parliament as they stand no matter how strongly the court suspected that it was not the real intention of Parliament. The *Hinchy* case involved careless drafting and Parliament quickly remedied the situation in the Finance Act 1960.

Golden Rule

The judge is still governed in the first instance by the words used. If these are clear and unambiguous they must be applied. However, where the literal rule would result in absurdity or inconsistency the judge may attempt to extend the meaning of the words used to reach a reasonable result. A court may avoid manifest absurdity in the construction of the statute by ascertaining the intention of a statute and varying or modifying its language. In those circumstances the court may select a secondary meaning but it must be a meaning that can be linguistically sustained by the words in dispute.

This approach found support in the case of *Becke* v *Smith* (1836) 2 M & W 191. The courts have been moving away from the literal rule to this type of construction. This fact was noted by the House of Lords in *Carter* v *Bradbeer* [1975] 1 WLR 665. The drawback is that a judge tends to take a subjective approach and arrives at a conclusion that is contrary to the literal interpretation of a statute. In the case of *Federal Steam Navigation Co. Ltd* v *Department of Trade and Industry* [1974] 1 WLR 505, the House of Lords interpreted the word 'or' as meaning 'and'. However, this was a majority decision and the minority dissented on the basis that the majority had taken an interpretation that was a flat rejection of the normal and grammatical exclusionary sense of the word used. The Oil in Navigable Waters Act 1955 had stated that 'the owner or master of the ship' should be punishable in the case of discharge of oil. The majority held that both the owner and master were liable to be prosecuted on the basis that 'or' in effect, included 'and'.

Mischief Rule

The mischief rule is the third approach to statutory interpretation. The Barons of the Exchequer in *Heydon's Case* (1584) 3 Co Rep 7 expounded four questions for ascertaining the meaning of statutes:

(a) What was the common law before the passing of the Act?

(b) What was the mischief and defect for which the common law did not provide?

(c)   What remedy has Parliament resolved and appointed to cure the disease?

(d)   What is the true reason of the remedy?

It is submitted that a more modern formulation of the mischief rule was laid down by Lord Diplock in *Jones* v *Wrotham Park Settled Estates* [1980] AC 74. Lord Diplock held that, first, there is to be a determination of the mischief the Act sought to remedy. It must be possible to determine this by considering the Act as a whole. Secondly, it must be apparent that the drafter and Parliament had by inadvertence overlooked and so had failed to deal with the eventuality, and thirdly, it must be possible for the courts to ascertain the words that could have been used by the drafter and approved by Parliament. It is important to note the observation of Lord Diplock that if the third requirement is not satisfied a court would be legislating and not determining the meaning of written law which Parliament had passed.

Purposive Approach

The purposive approach is wider than the mischief rule. At its widest it may involve a court looking to the purpose of an Act even where the words used are not ambiguous. That is where the distinction is between this rule and the golden and mischief rules. The golden and mischief rules are only to be resorted to when there is ambiguity in the wording of the statute. The purposive approach can be resorted to even though there is no ambiguity or absurdity on the face of the statute. The purposive approach is still in a developmental stage in English law. The purposive approach is the European method of statutory interpretation where the judge is not confined by the words used in a statutory provision but can consult extrinsic materials to assist in finding the meaning intended by the legislator. The British courts have had to interpret both European Community legislation and also domestic legislation designed to implement European Community legislation. In these situations they have taken a purposive approach. For example, in *Pickstone* v *Freemans plc* [1989] AC 66, the House of Lords held that it was permissible and necessary for the court to read words into inadequate domestic legislation in order to give effect to European Community law in relation to provisions relating to equal pay for work of equal value.

Conclusion

It should be clear from the above discussion that no principle of interpretation is paramount and that the process of interpretation is not merely a mechanical one but rather involves judicial creativity. The starting point ought always to be the natural meaning of the words used, and deviation from that standard is permitted to whatever degree is necessary according to the ambiguity or vagueness encountered. What the courts have tried to do is to minimise any overt evidence of judicial creativity.

QUESTION 4

Assess the impact and significance of *Pepper* v *Hart* [1993] AC 593.

Commentary

Pepper v *Hart* is potentially a very significant development concerning statutory interpretation. One has to consider the likely implications of the case on the traditional rules of statutory interpretation because it is arguably a purposive decision.

Suggested Answer

Traditionally judges have tended towards a narrow approach concerning statutory interpretation limiting themselves to the words of the statute. This means that they have made use of intrinsic aids to construction in preference to extrinsic aids. Intrinsic aids concern such internal evidence as the statute under consideration can provide through reference to the title of the Act, any preamble, and any schedules to it. Extrinsic aids can include dictionaries, textbooks, other statutes including the Interpretation Act 1978, reports, other Parliamentary papers, and, since *Pepper* v *Hart*, Hansard, the official report of Parliamentary debates.

The question that has to be considered is whether allowing the consultation of Hansard is a development of the purposive approach or is just part of the mischief rule but allowing another extrinsic aid to assist in the interpretation process.

This development has taken place under the heading of the mischief rule. The courts have allowed themselves to look at Law Commission reports, Royal Commission reports and the reports of other official commissions. However, the courts had a rule that Hansard could not be consulted. In *Pepper* v *Hart*, the House of Lords overturned this rule. In a majority decision, it was held that where the precise meaning of legislation was uncertain or ambiguous or where the literal meaning of an Act would lead to a manifest absurdity, the courts could refer to the reports of Parliamentary debates and proceedings as an aid to construing the meaning of the legislation.

Pepper v *Hart* is not intended to introduce a purposive approach to the interpretation of legislation. Hansard is to be considered only in the context of the mischief rule as a further method of finding out the mischief at which the particular legislation is aimed.

Another restriction is that it is likely that only statements made by a government Minister or some other sponsor responsible for the legislation will be considered as authoritative in setting out the mischief.

Facts and Reasoning of Pepper *v* Hart

There were two hearings of this case in the House of Lords and it was only on the second hearing, by using Hansard to aid the construction of a statute that the decision was made in favour of the taxpayers. Without the use of Hansard the case would have been decided in favour of the Inland Revenue. Malvern College operated a concessionary fee scheme under which members of staff could have their sons educated at the school for a fraction of the fees normally charged. The children had to meet the entrance requirements of the school and even then the scheme was wholly discretionary. No full fee payer was ever refused entry because of the presence of a teacher's child. For tax purposes, the benefit in kind had been assessed on the marginal costs to the school. The Inland Revenue argued that the benefit in kind should be a rateable proportion of all the general running expenses of the school. The relevant statutory provisions were ss. 61 and 63 of the Finance Act 1976, which are now the Income and Corporation Taxes Act 1988, ss. 154 and 156. Section 61 charged higher-paid employees and directors on the cash equivalent of any benefits in kind. The amount chargeable to tax was defined by s. 63(1) as the cost to the employer. It is s. 63(2) which was central to the argument. The relevant part is: '. . . the cost of a benefit is the amount of any expense incurred in or in connection with its provision, and . . . includes a proper proportion of any expense relating partly to the benefit and partly to other matters'.

There was a dispute about the meaning of the statute, and Hansard gave the answer. The statute on its face meant that taxpayers would be taxed on the basis of the market value of benefits in kind. However, in Parliament the Financial Secretary to the Treasury had been specifically questioned about the tax position of schoolteachers and had replied that the benefit would be assessed on the cost to the employer and not at market value. He further stated that this would be very small with regard to teachers.

Lord Mackay of Clashfern LC dissented on the use of Hansard but felt that he could come to the same result on the basis that the sons were only occupying surplus places and the right to do so was only discretionary. Lord Mackay objected to the use of Hansard because he thought that every question of statutory construction that comes before the courts would involve consultation of Hansard. Therefore the parties' legal advisers will have to study Hansard in practically every such case and this would increase the costs of litigation. Commenting on the case, Peter White, a solicitor and author of tax books, said that practitioners who consider statutory interpretation will have to consult Hansard 'if only to avoid negligence claims' ((1992) 136 SJ 1224 at p. 1225).

Lord Griffiths's view was that the courts now try to give effect to the true purpose of legislation. Lord Griffiths could not agree with the argument that consultation of Hansard would greatly increase costs and thought that modern technology would be helpful in this area. Further if the search resolves the ambiguity then it will save the costs of litigation because the matter would be resolved by considering Hansard.

Lord Browne-Wilkinson concluded that reference to Parliamentary materials would be possible in circumstances where:

(a) legislation is ambiguous or obscure, or leads to an absurdity;

(b) the material relied on consists of one or more statements by a Minister or other promoter of the Bill together if necessary with such other Parliamentary material as is necessary to understand such statements and their effect;

(c) the statements relied on are clear.

These preconditions were agreed upon by the majority. Lord Browne-Wilkinson stated that he would not be prepared to go further than this. If reference to Hansard had not been permissible in the instant case a literal construction of the statute would have meant the case would have been found in favour of the Inland Revenue.

After Pepper *v* Hart

In an article ([1994] Stat LR 10 reprinted in S. Lee and M. Fox, *Learning Legal Skills*, 2nd ed. (London: Blackstone Press, 1994)), Lord Lester quoted Professor St John Bates who has stated that the controls imposed by the Law Lords in *Pepper* v *Hart* have not been rigorously applied in practice. He found that courts are permitting reference to parliamentary material not only where legislation is ambiguous or obscure or leads to an absurdity. Lord Lester states 'Furthermore, courts have been looking at less than authoritative statements to the parliamentary record and adopting a relatively informal approach to referring to contextual parliamentary material'.

Conclusion

The impact of *Pepper* v *Hart* is that it permits more extrinsic material to be used in determining Parliamentary intention when applying the mischief rule. It comes close to the European purposive approach. The only difference between them is that the mischief rule says that Hansard may be consulted only when there is an ambiguity or unclearness, whereas the European purposive approach has no such precondition. It is therefore now a shorter step to the European purposive approach. This is probably why Lord Mackay dissented in *Pepper* v *Hart*. It is the judge who decides whether there is an ambiguity or unclearness and if counsel clearly shows that the Parliamentary debate shows a different intention from that expressed in the statute then that will be a justification for saying that the statute is unclear. Once the House of Lords in *Black-Clawson International Ltd* v *Papierwerke Waldhof-Aschaffenburg AG* [1975] AC 591 had permitted courts to look at official committee reports than there was no logical reason why Parliamentary statements by Ministers and other promoters of Bills could not also be considered. When *Pickstone* v *Freemans plc* [1989] AC 66 allowed the courts to consult Hansard with regard to British legislation enacting European Community obligations it left the law taking a different approach for different types of legislation. In those circumstances *Pepper* v *Hart* was inevitable.

QUESTION 5

After years of violent conduct in the UK and abroad by supporters of British football teams, the Sports (Prohibition of Alcohol Intoxicants) Act 1996 was passed on 21 March 1996. In introducing the Bill to Parliament, the Minister for Sport said that its purpose was 'to stop those hooligans who terrorise law-abiding citizens and have given the UK the worst name in the world'.

The Act is as follows:

An Act to reduce the dangers of football hooliganism.

1. It shall be an offence punishable by a fine not exceeding £20,000 for any person in the course of a business to supply any alcoholic beverage at any stadium, arena or other public place for consumption before, during or after any sporting event.

2. It shall be an offence punishable by a fine not exceeding £20,000 for any person to take into any stadium, arena or other public place any alcoholic beverage or similar substance.

The following matters have been referred to the Director of Public Prosecutions.

(a) On 21 March 1996 Danny went to an indoor tennis tournament at the Central Hall. He there consumed a bottle of ginger beer which he had bought a week earlier at a supermarket. The ginger beer contained 0.1 per cent of alcohol by volume.

(b) On 7 April, Ernie, an electrician, was called to repair the electrical connections to the lights in the changing room at West Ham football stadium, where an hour later, West Ham was to play Chelsea. On his way out, a tube of glue solvent fell out of his bag. It was found by Leeson, who was discovered with his friends sniffing the solvent in the stand at half-time.

(c) On 14 April, the day of the football match between England and Germany in Berlin, Gerry was observed in his off-licence shop in Dover selling tins of beer in large quantities to English fans who were about to catch the ferry to Europe. One of these fans, Harry, an electrician, missed the ferry and was seen on the following Saturday afternoon selling the same beer outside his local hockey club shortly before the kick off.

You are asked to advise the DPP, whether Danny, Ernie, Leeson, Gerry and Harry may be convicted of offences under the Act.

Suggested Answer

Danny

The Act would have come into operation on 21 March 1996 as it is stated that the Act was passed on that date and it may be assumed this was the date of

Royal Assent. By s. 4(b) of the Interpretation Act 1978 if there is no provision made for when an Act is to come into force then it does so at the beginning of the day on which it receives the Royal Assent.

The offence that Danny may be guilty of is one contrary to s. 2 of the Act, which makes it an offence for any person to 'take into any stadium, arena or other public place any alcoholic beverage or similar substance'. In interpreting s. 2, the following elements of the section have to be considered.

First, whether the Central Hall, where the indoor tennis tournament took place, can constitute a 'stadium, arena or other public place'. It can be argued that the Central Hall can constitute a public place. This will be the case as members of the public have access to it during the indoor tennis tournament. Since the words 'stadium' and 'arena' are particular words which are followed by the general words 'or other public place' it is arguable that the *eiusdem generis* rule would apply. This requires the general words to be limited to the 'genus' created by the particular words. However, as the words 'stadium' and 'arena' connote outdoor places where sporting events take place, it may follow that 'other public place' should only cover outdoor venues. However, it is submitted that the better view is that Parliament could not have intended the words 'other public place' to refer to places that are similar to the 'genus' but intended a wider meaning. Since any public place can come within the scope of the Act it is arguable that the *eiusdem generis* rule may not have any application. Lord Scarman in *Quazi* v *Quazi* [1980] AC 744 pointed out that the *eiusdem generis* rule may be a good servant but a bad master.

Secondly, it would be necessary to interpret the words 'alcoholic beverage or similar substance'. There would be an ambiguity here as the ginger beer Danny took to the tournament has only a small percentage of alcohol. It is arguable that since the words used are 'alcoholic beverage', any amount of alcohol in the beverage would be sufficient for the purpose of the Act. The ambiguity may be resolved by applying the mischief rule of construction. The rule as set out in *Heydon's Case* (1584) 3 Co Rep 7 requires the court where there is ambiguity to adopt the interpretation of a statute which will give effect to correcting the mischief in question. It would be legitimate to consider the preamble to the present statute to ascertain the mischief. Clearly it is to reduce football hooliganism. When enacting s. 2, Parliament clearly had in mind a situation where football fans would get drunk and misbehave. It is arguable that the alcohol content in the ginger beer is too negligible to have any intoxicating effect. A defendant might argue that the mischief rule should preclude s. 2 of the Act being used to cover sporting events such as an indoor tennis tournament because the preamble shows the Act is directed against football hooliganism. However, it can be argued that the court would not allow the preamble to create any ambiguity in the body of the Act. Section 2 does not state that the offence is in any way restricted to football matches. In *Powell* v *Kempton Park Racecourse Co. Ltd* [1899] AC 143, the Earl of Halsbury LC stated that if an enactment is clear and unambiguous then no preamble can qualify or cut down the enactment.

Since *Pepper* v *Hart* [1993] AC 593 it can be argued that Hansard should be consulted to see what statements the Minister made in Parliament. Here it is arguable that the legislation would lead to an absurdity if ginger beer comes within the provisions of the Act. The Minister said that the whole point of the Act was 'to stop those hooligans who terrorise law-abiding citizens and have given the UK the worst name in the world'. He may have said more than this but we are not told. This shows that the mischief that the Act was intended to remedy is hooligans behaving in a way that scares ordinary citizens. If young persons consume alcohol they have a tendency to become noisy and potentially aggressive. It can be argued that ginger beer would not do that and so the statute was not intended to cover the consumption of ginger beer.

Ernie

Ernie may be liable under s. 2 of the Act. The first issue is whether the glue solvent can constitute a 'similar substance' within the meaning of that section. It is arguable that the words 'similar substance' cannot be interpreted *eiusdem generis* as no genus is created by the phrase 'alcoholic beverage'. The words 'similar substance' could be interpreted to cover any substance such as a glue solvent as it can be argued that the solvent is capable of being 'sniffed' and has the same intoxicating effect as an alcoholic beverage. Assuming that the glue solvent comes within the phrase 'similar substance' the next point is whether the substance has been taken into any 'stadium, arena or other public place'. Ernie had gone to the showers at the West Ham stadium. It can be argued that the showers at the stadium would come within the word 'stadium'. There is an ambiguity here as it can also be argued that the showers in the West Ham stadium cannot come within the word 'stadium' as the section is directed against taking alcoholic beverages or similar substances to parts of the stadium where the sporting events take place. The mischief rule would be relevant here and it is submitted that the mischief that Parliament wanted to remedy in enacting s. 2 was to prevent alcoholic beverages or similar substances being taken into part of the stadium where the sporting events take place and where supporters are present.

Leeson

As for the offence Leeson may be charged with, the first point to note is that sniffing in the stands is not an offence. Section 2, however, is relevant here as, assuming the solvent is considered a 'similar substance' the question would be whether Leeson has taken it into the stadium, arena or other public place. It can be argued that the stands would come within the definition of 'stadium'.

Gerry

The offence to be considered here would be one contrary to s. 1 of the Act. Gerry was clearly selling the beer in his off-licence. On the literal interpretation of s. 1 the 'supply' of any alcoholic beverage has to be at any 'stadium, arena or public place'. It can be argued that the off-licence would not come within the scope of 'stadium, arena or public place'. The court, on the other hand, may be persuaded to apply the mischief rule. The modern formulation of this rule is found in a speech by Lord Diplock in *Jones* v *Wrotham Park Settled Estates* [1980] AC 74 where his lordship stated three conditions that have to be satisfied:

(a)   It must be possible to determine from a consideration of the Act as a whole precisely what the mischief was that it was the purpose of the Act to rectify.

(b)   It must be apparent that Parliament had inadvertently overlooked and omitted to deal with the mischief.

(c)   The court must be able to state with certainty what were the additional words that Parliament could have included.

The court may conclude that the mischief is to prevent supporters taking alcoholic beverages into a stadium and so supply at any place must be prohibited. However, such a construction, it is submitted, would not be correct since the words in s. 2 are without any ambiguity and the courts should not read into the Act words that have not been included. The next point is whether Gerry can commit an offence contrary to s. 1 if the football match takes place in Germany and not in the UK. Here there is an uncertainty as s. 1 is not clear since it refers to only a sporting event. The court can resolve this uncertainty by applying the mischief rule. The speech by the Minister in Parliament may be helpful here. Since the case of *Pepper* v *Hart* [1993] AC 593 it is possible to consider what he said in Parliament to resolve this uncertainty. The Minister was certainly concerned with the behaviour of English football fans overseas. Thus s. 1 could be utilised to deal with the present situation.

Harry

The main issue here would be whether Harry is supplying the beer in the course of a business. Since Harry is an electrician he is not in the business of selling beer. However, it is submitted that the phrase 'in the course of a business' when read with 'supply' could refer to anyone who is selling an alcoholic beverage with a view to making a profit which would be enough to make the supply 'in the course of a business'. Applying the golden rule it could be argued that it is absurd to conclude that Harry is supplying in the 'course of a business' and that the Act here would provide more convenience if the words 'in the course of a business' were interpreted to apply to someone who is actually in the business of selling alcoholic beverages. As this approach may result in the judge giving his views on the policy of Parliament such an approach may not be acceptable (see *Duport Steels Ltd* v *Sirs* [1980] 1 WLR 142).

Index